Practices of Resilient Companies

Practices of Resilient Companies

Overcome Disruption with Compassion, Collaboration, and Knowledge

Ron Robinson

BUSINESS EXPERT PRESS
Leader in applied, concise business books

Practices of Resilient Companies:
Overcome Disruption with Compassion, Collaboration, and Knowledge

Cover design by Cassandra Kronstedt

Interior design by S4Carlisle Publishing Services, Chennai, India

First published in 2026 by
Business Expert Press, LLC
222 East 46th Street, New York, NY 10017
www.businessexpertpress.com

ISBN-13: 978-1-63742-962-4 (hardcover)
ISBN-13: 978-1-63742-948-8 (paperback)
ISBN-13: 978-1-63742-949-5 (e-book)

Human Resource Management and Organizational Behavior Collection

First edition: 2026

10 9 8 7 6 5 4 3 2 1

EU SAFETY REPRESENTATIVE
Mare Nostrum Group B.V.
Mauritskade 21D
1091 GC Amsterdam
The Netherlands
gpsr@mare-nostrum.co.uk

Dedication

This book is dedicated to the memory of David Natysin. I had the privilege of serving Dave and his team of directors as they worked together to make the Washington, DC region of McDonald's the top region in the U.S. market. Dave's generosity and loyalty to his people became a part of my life and my values. When I pass on and find Dave with his friends in heaven, I look forward to joining him for a Big Mac value meal.

Description

Practices of Resilient Companies: Overcome Disruption with Compassion, Collaboration, and Knowledge provides the antidote for what ails companies in today's mayhem. It describes ongoing disruptions in our lives and leaders who have led their organizations to higher heights during this century's unpredictability. The author provides research and insightful stories for readers seeking to anticipate and react to chaos. Readers will learn how climate disasters increase in intensity and frequency while social issues abound as seven million people take to the streets. The book also discusses political actions that threaten to trigger viral outbreaks, inflation, and recession, as well as the expanding reach of social media and artificial intelligence, which cause conflict and create barriers between companies and customers.

The book is divided into four parts, each containing stories of leaders who have improved efficiency in their operations to counter climate disasters, strengthened their financial margins to cope with political actions, changed cultures to retain and stabilize their workforce during social complexity and unrest, and devised processes for delighting their customers while wrestling with constantly changing technology.

The ability to design strategies that anticipate disruption determines whether business leaders and owners fail, survive, or thrive. Readers will discover an enhanced business strategy that would help bring their organizations together in order to navigate today's evolving ecosystems. The process enables readers to chart their possibilities, enhance the performance of the four components of their companies, and thrive in today's unpredictable economy. I believe you will find the stories herein enlightening and that they will motivate you to develop resilient practices for thriving in today's changing world.

Contents

List of Tables, Boxes and Figure

Tables

Boxes

Figure

Review Quotes

"Ron has incredible experience and skills. His model for success is worth learning and applying. Highly recommend!"—**Kenneth Flynt, Associate Dean, College of Business, Western Carolina University**

"Thanks, Ron! This is something I am incredibly proud of and thankful that I committed to going through your program! We are reaching milestones that have never been achieved in the history of this agency, and it all started when we started working together."—**Tyler Richardson, Tennessee Agency Manager, COUNTRY Financial**

"Ron has served as a speaker for several of our business meetings. He never disappoints and always delvers a stellar, to the point and meaningful presentation. He is a well diverse speaker on a variety of topics that any size business can benefit from."—**CeCe Hipps, President, Haywood Chamber of Commerce**

"Ron's organizational skills and his ability to keep everyone focused and moving forward brought our organization from surviving to thriving."—**Linda Potter, Jackson County Public School Librarian**

"It tells you what not to do, what to do and shows you how to do it. It is a great book."—**Adam Bridges, Waynesville Farm Bureau Agency Manager**

"Ron is a positive leader who knows how to help others be their best. I've worked with him in Jackson County and been nothing but impressed. Two thumbs up!!!"—**Bill Ogletree, PhD, Communications Department Head, Health and Human Sciences, WCU**

Personal Thoughts on Personal Resilience

I have enjoyed life, suffered, loved, and lost, loved again during a long and rewarding life. During my journey I found that life consists of body, mind, soul, and spirit. I attempt to balance my life by paying attention to all four components. I hope you discover some of the truths I learned while careening through life and find tools and talents to thrive during the unpredictable turbulence of this churning century.

As I learned, Body involves how we care for ourselves and our physical well-being. In business it concerns how we care for the body of our operations in our companies and the well-being of how things function. Mind relates to our intellect, either personally or collectively. In business and families, the ability to manage numbers and investments plays a critical role. Spirit is the energy we put into our lives at home and work or in retirement. In business our workforce creates a spirit that can raise us out of despair or take us down. Soul concerns our sense of ethics and morality within our families, companies, and communities. It leads to our demise if overlooked and to greater success when it remains at the top of our hearts. All four components helped me become more resilient and has assisted many companies do the same.

Take Care

I have a choice when I wake up in the morning. I can choose to talk myself down and look at a half-empty cup of coffee, or to anticipate a great day with a topped-off cup of perfectly blended coffee with whipped cream. I have benefited from counseling and medications for depression and diabetes. I found a partner who compliments and strengthens me every day. My wife, Judy, is why I write books and poetry and wake up with a smile. My workouts of biking, running, and hiking help to stimulate ideas for a healthy life and being competitive with other consulting firms.

Be Honest

It is OK to be human. The weight of the world lifted from my shoulders the day I took the blame for something that was going wrong. I was assigned to cover our real estate office one Saturday and came in late. An agent criticized me. Normally I would have made an excuse. For some reason I said, "Yep, my bad and it won't happen again." I felt so much better. Basketball players point to themselves when they make an error in a game and say, "My bad."

These lessons apply not only to ourselves but also to business operations as well as our persons as we plan actions to make our companies efficient and responsive to change.

Work Very Hard

Work to find better-paying jobs. Never be satisfied with what you are earning. Generate extra income and invest the money you earn. I started selling real estate and working for a nonprofit. I was barely making a living. I took an assignment with FEMA (Federal Emergency Management Agency) to bring in more income. As I increased my income, I saved enough money to buy a foreclosed property. On weekends and evenings, I renovated the house and sold it, doubling my investment. I found another property in bad shape, negotiated hard, and purchased it at a good price. I renovated it over six months and used it for long-term rental income before selling it in a hot housing market. When I save $5,000, I invest in the stock market. I know market values rise and fall, and I keep cash on hand to purchase stock when values drop. That is how I describe hard work.

Stand Tall

I used to be more passive when challenged, but no more. After three years of clawing back after losing my well-paid job, home, and all my savings, I learned to take care of every penny and to fight back when challenged. I learned how it feels when someone is at their lowest

In 2001, I lost my consulting job in Atlanta and moved back to the mountains. I sold real estate and worked for a nonprofit in Asheville, North Carolina. My nonprofit job paid barely enough to live on, but it had health insurance. Our home in Atlanta was up for sale but had no takers. I decided to sell it myself since our realtor was having no success. I prepared leaflets and advertised our home for auction in shopping centers. My realtor said it would not work. On the day of the auction, one person visited and offered us $40,000 more than our asking price. We sold just before Wachovia foreclosed on us.

A year later, I met with the executive director of the nonprofit and explained how I could help in other areas of the organization. Within a week, I received an assignment to run a program and turn it around. My income nearly tripled. Another company visited our program, and I learned they needed staff. I joined them and increased my income again. Then I found my love, consulting, and increased my income once again. If I had not stood up for myself, I would not have pulled myself out of poverty.

Income

The Honey Baked Ham Company is the perfect example: It offers its franchisees three income streams, including ham sales, lunch menus, and catering. I have developed several sources of income including property rental, book sales, consulting services, and stock dividends. Your sources of income will be different, and it takes years to generate enough resources to invest and create three or more streams of income. A business owner I know uses his office space during the week and rents it out on weekends. Develop your vision for three income streams and work toward that vision. A vision helps motivate us to work toward a cause and look forward to each day.

I have found that my lessons prove fruitful as I assist companies improve financial performance during the uncertainty of today's government policy changes impacting businesses and communities.

Winners Listen

A workshop participant expressed frustration as we discussed showing empathy. His need was to win every argument. To him, showing empathy was agreeing with the other person's point of view. He felt a deep compulsion to win when debating with someone. His face scrunched up as he accepted the notion that others had just as much right to their ideas as he did to his. On reflection he explained to our class that most of his conflicts were with his wife. And now he seeks to approach ideas from her point of view. He had a big smile as he shared his experiences with us.

Goals and Rewards

I worked my way through college selling dictionaries. My sales manager at the Southwestern Company in Nashville, Ted Welch, observed that I was the most goal-oriented person he had ever met. Setting goals was how I received the President's Award with the company. When I lost everything after the attacks of September 11 and had to start over, setting income goals helped me move up the income ladder. I kept telling myself, *I will never be poor again*, and focused on my next goal. That process pulled me out of the darkness and into the light. Anticipating the achievement of each goal kept big smiles on my face as I met each one. When selling real estate in Asheville, I determined rewards for every sale. For small sales, I had a special meal at Boston Market. My big goal was to save enough money to buy a road bike, a LeMond black beauty. Now I take Judy out to her favorite restaurant when I get a consulting contract or a book deal. Always combine rewards with goal achievement at home and with your businesses. It is how we make work fun!

Smell the Roses

Early in my life I became addicted to work and money. I spent more time with clients than my family. I knew my clients better than my wife and children. I failed to set boundaries for time at work and with my family. When the job vanished, I struggled to engage with my family. Now I take time to enjoy hikes with Judy and our dog. I have reconnected with my children and Judy's children and she has built relationships with mine. I enjoy workouts and spending time in the mornings watching birds at our bird feeders.

Good in Others

No matter the conflict or stress they create, there is always something good in other people. When we recognize the good in others, we find good in ourselves. For example, I invested in rental property for much of my career. For the most part I found renters to be delightful and happy to have affordable housing. A few renters, however, could be demanding, would damage property, or could be obnoxious. But there was good to be found in them. One family consisted of a passive-aggressive mother and a resistant-to-rules husband. At this property dogs and cats were not allowed. Without permission two dogs were brought to the property. They scratched refinished wood floors and dug up the yard. Somehow, family members tore two kitchen cabinet doors off their hinges. I was upset but reminded myself this family had weathered many storms in their lives and were raising three beautiful and bright children. I admired their fight and resilience.

Respect Others

When working with a nonprofit, my responsibilities included finding jobs and coaching people with developmental disabilities. I was fortunate to serve a young woman with engaging eyes and a winning smile. Her job was to take soiled sheets and towels to the laundry and stock closets with clean sheets and towels at a resort. One day, several golfers gathered with us waiting for the elevator, and I noticed a man staring at my client. To redirect his gaze I asked, "How are you today?" He gave me a cold look and replied, "What is it to you?" I refrained from saying what I was thinking. I have never forgotten the arrogance of that golfer and the lesson he taught me.

These lessons come from my heart and experiences growing through life and hard times. Many of these lessons keep me positively focused and willing to stand up and fight circumstances that, in the past, could bring me down. Taking time to reflect has become my way to stay in the light and away from the black hole I fell into. Each of us has lessons we have learned and I wish you the best as you reflect on your life's lessons and the stories I share with you.

Introduction

I was asked by CeCe Hipps, president of the Haywood Chamber of Commerce, how businesses survive as ecosystems evolve. I presented a business model that helps clients recover quickly from change or disruption, that is, become resilient. *Practices of Resilient Companies: Overcome Disruption with Compassion, Collaboration, and Knowledge* provides the antidote that is ideally timed and positioned for companies facing chaos, confusion, and uncertainty in today's marketplace. It describes how chief executive officers (CEOs), management teams and business owners challenge assumptions with a strategy that anticipates and prepares for the disruptions to their ecosystems. The chaos and destruction in 2020 increased the tempo of change with four disruptions caused by climate destruction, society's complexity, political actions, and technology change.

The theme is about how businesses adapt to these disruptions based on how leaders and managers make assumptions about risk and create growth strategies. Studies have documented that 70 percent of businesses fail within 10 years. Successful leaders focus on integrity, as well as the human and technical components of their businesses, and become facilitators. They create highly competitive organizations in the whirlwind of today's ever-changing economy. An Internet search delivers multiple pages listing leadership and management theory and advice. You may have read many of them. So what makes this book worth reading?

First, you will become part of the 30 percent of leaders and managers who learn what I have learned helping businesses achieve higher levels of success. While most management books focus on the steps to help the reader improve, this book offers a comprehensive view of today's changing ecosystem and the tools and talents used by managers who excel during adversity.

Second, I usually only get through half the books I read. This book will be concise for those who read half a book as I do but expect to learn the whole story. I enjoy storytelling but will refrain from reliving more stories than necessary to illustrate lessons learned.

Third, management teams focus on the present. They put their heads down and plow ahead responding to challenges of the moment. They overlook lessons of the past and fail to anticipate what may be looming in their futures. This book provides a roadmap leading them to a brighter future.

Fourth, this is written to help readers become clearer eyed about their assumptions regarding four disruption facing companies, nonprofits, and communities. Concepts are organized into four parts within the book discussing disruptions within business ecosystems, a strategy for responding to disruptions followed by actions taken by companies to react and succeed in spite of the challenges they encounter.

Disruptions remain a reality as investors on Wall Street and stock markets react unpredictability and the future certainly appears uncertain for U.S. and world economies. To succeed in turbulence, management teams who possess ambition, integrity, and a hunger to tackle problems build resilience into their companies. They consider internal vulnerabilities and external disruption as opportunities. I hope you enjoy their stories using compassion, collaboration, and knowledge for building great organizations that excel in today's uncertain world.

PART 1

Disruption

Before considering any change to the manner in which we live our lives or run our companies we must have reasons to change. Personally, in our communities and in our companies, four very good reasons compel us to adapt. Disruptions including climate disasters, social complexity, political actions, and technology change continually impact the manner in which we live and work. Achieving awareness of these disruptive forces is the first step when adapting to today's uncertainty and building highly resilient companies and communities.

CHAPTER 1

Climate Disasters

Nature's impact on economic wealth and destruction through the assumptions and facts considered by how country, town, and urban entities efficiently develop and exchange goods and services. Our changing environment is creating risks to our livelihoods. This chapter describes the impact of climate disasters on our companies and communities.

The hottest year on record was 2024. With 11 dead, more than 12,000 structures destroyed or damaged and 150,000 residents under evacuation order, the siege of wildfires in the Los Angeles area in January 2025 has the potential of being the costliest wildfire disaster in American history, according to UCLA climate scientist Daniel Swan.[1]

> Environmental disruptions impact our operations in a host of ways. Flooding handicaps the flow of goods, generates havoc in our places of business, and creates extensive damage that takes years for companies and communities to fully recover. Extreme storms, wildfires, and droughts are leading to stress and conflicts within communities and companies as they execute their plans. The conflict over access to water in the Midwest is just one example of increasing battles over resources as our climate changes.

I learned from Daniel how floods and wildfires feed each other. When an area floods, water nourishes the land and stimulates plant growth. When droughts occur, plants die and become dry, providing fuel for the

---

[1]Daniel is an alumnus of the University of California, Davis (BS, Atmospheric Science) and of Stanford University (PhD, Earth System Science), and completed his postdoctoral work at UCLA. He is also the author of the widely read Weather West blog (weatherwest.com), which provides real-time perspectives on California weather and climate, and can be found on Twitter (@Weather_West), Bluesky (@WeatherWest), and YouTube (@WeatherWest).

next wildfire. After the wildfire devastates the community, storms occur and the cycle begins again.

Changing Climate

The Pigeon River in Canton, a mill town in the heart of North Carolina's Great Smoky Mountains, burst its banks on August 17, 2021, when Tropical Storm (TS) Fred roared into the area from Florida's Gulf Coast. TS Fred was one of 20 climate disasters in the United States in 2021. We may think we are protected from such catastrophes; TS Fred proved us wrong, as major damage was inflicted on western North Carolina once again. Hurricanes Frances and Ivan had also devastated the community in 2004. Excerpts from reporting on TS Fred by Blue Ridge Public Radio (BPR) offer a reminder of how communities are impacted.

> (5:39 p.m. EDT) Canton football stadium flooded on August 17th. At a press briefing earlier Wednesday, emergency services director Travis Donaldson said about 30 people were still unaccounted for. The Pigeon River in Canton rose almost 17 feet in less than 10 hours Tuesday, flooding downtown and surrounding areas.
>
> In neighboring Transylvania County, initial damage estimates in the county top $2 million, with 25 structures said to be damaged or uninhabitable, plus five roadways with serious damage. A train trestle in the Pisgah National Forest was moved two feet by floodwaters, according to officials.
>
> Yesterday afternoon, the French Broad almost set a new record level in Transylvania County when it passed 14 feet around 5:30 p.m. The record in that portion of the river is 14.9 feet.
>
> State Route 276 is closed because of flooding.
>
> (6:30 p.m.) Emergency crews had to rescue trapped motorists after flooding stranded cars along Smokey Park Highway in Candler.
>
> (7:00 p.m.) I-40 westbound is down to one lane at mile marker 36.5.

(8:30 p.m.) US 19/23 is closed in both directions due to a landslide near Bridge Road near Canton. US 70 is closed in Swannanoa because of flooding.

"Searches Continue in Haywood & Transylvania as More Rain Looms," BPR News, August 17, 2021

Zeb Smathers, Canton's mayor, was asked about his experience during TS Fred's visit. The mayor is a big man who wears dark-blue suits and has thick black hair accenting sparkling blue eyes and a reluctant smile. He leaned forward as he described in a deep and deliberate voice the hour and half he had to react. "It came out of nowhere, a monster!" he exclaimed. "We heard 60 people died in Cruso." In news updates he learned that the flood had killed six people. He described his call to Washington, DC, for help, the FEMA's red tape, Governor Cooper's visit, and Canton's fire department, police department, and service agencies pulling together to help. He described the overwhelming force of the flood and its impact on roads, farms, and lives. He acknowledged the need to review forest management techniques, the buildup of debris along the banks and in the river, and to dredge the river to remove debris that was a cause of this flood. He described how the Internet and social media increased speed of communication compared to the 2004 flood. The technology helped to coordinate agencies and volunteers and bring people together to help one another during and after the disaster.

According to the mayor, some of these same people are now slowing the changes needed to avoid another crisis. They are still rebuilding and recovering from the 2004 storm. "It is all about the people; without people, we have nothing." Zeb's lessons include building remediation into new development, anticipating the next apocalypse—fire or water—assembling and using the skills available around you. He also emphasized the importance of ensuring clarity of roles and responsibilities. People see what is going on around them, so it is essential to communicate with them regarding those experiences.

Zeb's father, Pat, was mayor of Canton during the floods in 2004. It is no secret where Zeb got his size and thick hair. Pat is a bit larger and taller than his son and has thick gray hair, the same sparkling eyes, and a more relaxed and easier smile. He recalled the difficulty of declaring a state of emergency after being overwhelmed by two hurricanes: Frances and Ivan. "It was hard to say we can't handle it by ourselves," he said. The words I heard him repeat were "new opportunity." He explained that after the storms subsided and water retreated back to the river, they began moving homes and businesses out of the floodplain. They redirected water flow away from the town and cleared debris from the river. They converted the cleared areas to parks and gardens. "There is more quality of life here now, a better place to live. Because of our work, the 2021 flood created much less property damage," Pat said. Their projects were completed in 2012, eight years after the flood.

I reviewed with Pat the alarming frequency of extreme storms in our mountains and asked when he expected the next flood. He cocked his head to one side as he reflected and said, "10 to 15 years." I suggested that we would be lucky if we make it more than five years, based on current weather trends. After our meeting, as I walked back to my truck, I thought about how lucky people in Canton must feel having the support of mayors Zeb and Pat Smathers during their times of trial. I also felt fortunate to have met them and learned their lessons: Zeb's advice to "Build remediation into everything" and his reminder, "It's all about the people"—and Pat's advice to keep looking for opportunities in the aftermath of a disaster and to do the best we can when disasters come our way.

TS Fred was the second to last in a series of extreme weather events in western North Carolina. Hurricanes traveled from the Gulf Coast in 1940, 1977, 2004, 2018, 2022, and 2024. Both Frances and Ivan hit in 2004. The alarming statistic is the increased frequency with which these climate disasters are occurring: 37 years between the first and second flood; 27 years between the second and third occurrence; 14 years between the third and fourth; and just three years between the last two episodes. Hurricane Helene's destruction throughout Western North Carolina in 2024 follows only two years since the last hurricane. Why are these happening? Climate change, coupled with geography, weather patterns, road placement, farm management, tree removal, housing development, and community conflicts, makes a bad situation worse. No matter where we live, these issues contribute to the effects of climate disasters.

Hurricane Helene, one of the deadliest U.S. storms of the 21st century, roared through Western North Carolina on Friday, September 27, 2024. The storm is credited with more than 100 deaths, thousands of homes destroyed, and tens of thousands more damaged by 1,000-year floods and landslides. Millions of North Carolinians lost access to critical services like water and sewer, electricity, telecommunications, and health care facilities. Thirty-nine counties were impacted making up 40 percent of the state's population. Thousands of miles of roads and bridges were damaged, cutting communities off and limiting egress for residents and entrance by essential response and recovery teams. Estimates of damage are more than $59.6 billion across the state.

The experiences of the mountain people in Western North Carolina are repeated across our country and the world as our climate changes. In a Pew survey conducted by Brian Kennedy and Alec Tyson (December 9, 2024), titled "How Americans View Climate Change and Policies to Address The Issues," reports that 69 percent of those surveyed say large businesses and corporations are doing too little to help reduce the effects of climate change. Sixty percent of those surveyed viewed state elected officials as doing too little, while 57 percent of those surveyed thought energy industry leaders are not doing enough. The survey also revealed that 57 percent say ordinary Americans are doing too little to reduce the effects of climate change.

Human-caused climate change will make extreme weather events more frequent and more damaging, based on current trends and patterns. Climate disasters averaged three per year from 2000 to 2020. Wildfires wiped out entire towns, flooding in the Midwest destroyed crops and communities, hurricanes on the Gulf and Atlantic coasts led to billions of dollars in damage, and warm ocean waters off the coast of Alaska disrupted the fishing economy. An insurance carrier withdrew from California due to increasing wildfire destruction. Since 2020, climate disasters in the United States have accelerated at an alarming pace—from 22 in 2020 to a record 28 in 2023, including floods, droughts, and fires. The United States saw 27 climate disasters totaling $1 billion or more in collective damages in 2024. Most Americans believe that climate change is happening, while debate by the two political parties, environmental groups, and fossil fuel interests continues, blocking progress. In the meantime, temperatures keep increasing, rainfall becomes more intense, wildfires increase, and seashores get washed away, causing population migration northward to more temperate climates.

Making Situations Worse

While our actions have created this new world climate, how we make situations worse is described through the story of a small mountain village. In this village, a family lived in a charming cottage, painted a wood-tone color with flower boxes of bright-red geraniums under its front windows. The yard, covered with grass and shaded by mighty Oak and Maple trees, sloped toward a stream. When sitting on the front porch, the family enjoyed the melody of the cascading water winding its way downstream. Every spring, heavy rains energized the stream, water roaring to the top of its banks. One morning the family heard a loud rumbling noise. As the noise grew louder, they peered outside and panicked as they watched in horror a wave of water cascading toward them. They escaped just before their home was washed away. The soothing stream turned into a major disruption when a housing development upstream paved the parking lot. Without open ground to absorb the rainfall, water had nowhere to go except downhill.

The lesson learned is that our climate is changing at an accelerating pace. Too many communities and companies ignore renewable energy options having a smaller footprint on climate change. While building codes exist that provide for more resilient structures, communities are slow to adopt and enforce the changes. Is it possible that leaders will recognize that the future is here and applying building codes and using fossil fuels like it was yesterday is no longer an option?

Five Questions

1. The hottest year on record is:
   A. 2020
   B. 2024
   C. 2023
   D. 2007

2. Climate disruptions are:
   A. Less intense
   B. Normal occurrences
   C. More intense
   D. Fake news

3. What year did climate disasters increase in frequency?
   A. 2010
   B. 2015
   C. 2020
   D. 2024

4. Climate disasters averaged three per year between which years?
   A. 2000 and 2005
   B. 2000 and 2010
   C. 2000 and 2015
   D. 2000 and 2020

5. Climate disasters are caused by:
   A. Outdated building codes
   B. Political/community resistance to change
   C. Corporate opposition to renewable energy
   D. All of the above

CHAPTER 2

Social Complexity

The manner in which managers communicate, discipline, and motivate a limited supply of diverse people and values matters if we are to build resilient companies. Changes in the composition of our populations are impacting how we recruit, retain, and grow our workforce and how we communicate with customers. This chapter will share data to highlight that we need to do a better job of cooperating with and supporting those with whom we work. While data can be boring, you may find this information particularly helpful when thinking through policies and practices in your workplace.

The Economics Daily of the U.S. Bureau of Labor Statistics in its report (September 8, 2025) states, "There were 7.2 million unemployed people in July 2025 and, on the last business day, 7.2 million job openings. This yielded a ratio of unemployed people to job openings of 1.0 for July." Since the 2020 pandemic, our workforce has been depleted, with over 28 million baby boomers retiring and more than three million deaths reported in the United States that year. The labor shortage is compounded by Congress failing to adequately supplement our labor supply with immigrants. So when someone complains that people do not want to work, gently remind them the supply of people is limited and Congress has not created immigration policies to address workforce needs of companies.

We are now experiencing what some would call a "frozen" labor market. Hiring has slowed, workers have stopped job shopping in an uncertain economy, and layoffs remain rare because hiring managers face challenges replacing lost talent. In such a labor market companies must optimize the potential within workplaces consisting of greater cultural, generational, and gender representation.

Cultural Differences

The manner in which various backgrounds, interests, and experiences are managed plays a direct role in how well companies perform. The BLS reports on the workforce's cultural composition in 2024. Of 168,104 million employed people, men comprise 52.9 percent of the workforce, women comprise 47.1 percent. White worker participation declined from 76.5 percent in 2023 to 75.9 percent in 2024. Hispanic participation increased from 18.5 percent in 2023 to 19.6 percent in 2024. African American participation increased from 12.8 percent in 2023 to 13.1 percent in 2024. Asian/Native American/Alaskan/Hawaiian and Pacific Islander participation moved from 6.9 to 11 percent in 2024. How these groups are compensated reveals a disparity in management practices both toward genders and ethnic groups. The median weekly earnings of full-time hourly and salaried workers have changed from 2023 to Q2 2025 as follows: Asian men $1,635 to $1,759; Asian women from $1,299 to $1,363; White men from $1,225 to $1,357; White women from $1,021 to $1,100; Black men from $970 to $1,053; Black women from $889 to $942; Hispanic men from $915 to $1,005; Hispanic women from $800 $880. While different jobs pay differently, the question should be asked, "Why are those earning less not developed by their employers to earn more?"

The Pew Research Center reports on how various ethnic groups view their work environments. Discrimination varies by race: 8 percent of white workers, 20 percent of Hispanic workers, 25 percent of Asian workers, and 41 percent of Black workers report being treated unfairly because of their race or ethnicity by an employer when it comes to hiring, pay, or promotion. While 23 percent of employed women reported discrimination, only 10 percent of men did. From a Pew report, "How Much Discrimination Do Americans Say Groups Face in the U.S.?" (May 20, 2025), we learn that nearly three-quarters of Americans say Black people (74 percent) and Hispanic people (72 percent) face at least some discrimination. About two-thirds (66 percent) say Asian people face a lot of or some discrimination, 65 percent say immigrants who are legally in this country also face a lot of or some bias. Nearly two-thirds of adults (64 percent) say women face at least some discrimination, with far fewer (34 percent) saying the same about men (Table 2.1).

Table 2.1 Workforce participation and discrimination

Group	Workforce participation	Weekly compensation	Experience discrimination
Asian	11.0%	Men: $1,759 Women: $1,363	25%
Black	13.1%	Men: $1,053 Women: $942	41%
Hispanic	19.6%	Men: $1,005 Women: $880	20%
White	75.9%	Men: $1,330 Women: $1,078	8%

Discrimination is not only perceived by the public and ethnic groups; evidence-based reporting describes how it is increasing based on the U.S. Equal Employment Opportunity Commission (EEOC)'s 2024 annual report. The EEOC received 88,531 new charges of discrimination in fiscal year 2024, more than 9 percent increase over charges filed in fiscal year 2023. The EEOC received more than 553,000 calls from the public, an almost 6 percent increase from 2023 and 90,000 e-mails, an increase of almost 5 percent from 2023. In fiscal year 2023 the EEOC resolved 35 sexual harassment lawsuits. In Kingman, Arizona, a McDonald's franchise owner was charged with supervisors, managers, and coworkers knowing about unwanted touching, offensive comments, sexual advances, and intimidation of younger workers but not doing anything about it. The owner settled the lawsuit for $1,997,500.

Retaliation lawsuits numbered 56. Pacific Culinary and CB Foods were taken to court by the EEOC, charged with ongoing harassment and retaliation and constructive discharge. When employees complained of harassment to managers, the harassment intensified, causing the employees to quit. The companies agreed to pay $245,000 and furnish injunctive relief to settle the lawsuit. Boeing was also caught up in retaliation complaints, as its chief admitted; the company retaliated against whistleblowers participating in Senate hearings.

Generational Differences

In interviews and observations with clients it has become evident that younger workers (up to the age of 40) are frustrated by not being heard for their ideas. They experience older workers viewing them as being overly concerned with their phones, technology, and play time outside of work. In his article "How Shifting Demographics Are Changing the Workforce," Steve Boese of H3HR writes,

> Looking at the Generations more closely, we see that each is evolving, and the combined effects impact the overall labor force, and trickle down to effect localities, industries, and individual organizations
>
> (https://www.h3hr.com/labor-market-focus-how-shifting -demographics-are-changing-the-workforce/; August 5, 2024)

Baby Boomers (1946 to 1964) value company loyalty and long-term employment, teamwork, paying one's dues, and sacrificing personal goals for success at work. Approximately 19 percent of the workforce will continue to retire, leading to a decrease in their representation. Some will remain employed due to financial necessity or personal choice.

Generation X (1965 to 1980) value independence and individuality, prefer working with younger managers and innovative coworkers, and embrace new technologies. This generation comprises nearly 36 percent of the workforce; many are holding management and leadership positions in their organizations, or having built their own businesses. The older members of Gen X are approaching 60 years old and are beginning to contemplate or even transition into retirement.

Millennials (1981 to 1996) value responsibility, the quality of their manager, challenging work experience, development and opportunities for future growth, fun at work, and work–life balance. Millennials are the largest generation in the workforce comprising over 40 percent of those employed. They are moving into senior roles in their organizations while many juggle caregiving for children and parents.

Generation Z (1997 to 2012) shaped by their experiences during the COVID-19 pandemic are mindful of their mental and emotional health. They share with Millennials their value for balance between work and personal time. They value diversity of cultures and genders, receiving personalized attention, being treated as individuals, encouraging creativity of thought, and being viewed as digital device specialists. A little over 6 percent of the workforce, this generation will increase their labor participation over the next 5 to 10 years. They can be expected to bring new talents and ideas regarding technology and digital innovation.

How can a workforce with as many as five generations make or break company performance? Research by Professor Dr. Uschi Backes-Gellner and Stephan Veen of the University of Zurich's Institute for Strategy and Business Economics revealed that a workforce consisting of multiple generations can create greater relationship problems, communication misunderstandings, and significant staff turnover in companies with standard procedures and production processes for routine tasks (e.g., bicycle wheels). However, companies involved in non-routine tasks, such as software development, achieve benefits for collaboration and innovation when developing unique products and services. The disadvantages described for routine-task companies exist with non-routine work as well, but the benefits of more informed decisions are greater. The researchers reported that "in innovative companies a 10% increase in age heterogeneity increases annual productivity by approximately 3.5%." Regardless of the nature of the company, the challenges presented by multiple generations are effectively managed in the same manner as managing multiple cultures.

Social changes in communities drive changes in the workforce and labor supply. These changes stretch the ability and creativity of management teams. Further, the woke movement discourages acknowledgment of the unique needs of various cultures and generations, creating stress on conventional management when recruiting, retaining, and growing today's workforce. Missteps by managers can be costly when treating separate groups differently regarding pay and work assignments. When managers listen and facilitate involved decision making with their workers, companies improve their bottom lines and have happier employees. Going forward, those organizations that develop tools, talents, and strategies for their management teams to pull people together and collaborate will be part of a total solution for resolving discriminatory practices, increasing production and efficiency and building resilience organizations.

Five Questions

1. The supply of labor in the United States is
   A. Increasing
   B. Remains the same
   C. Decreasing
   D. None of the above
2. In today's labor market
   A. Workers are quitting at a higher rate
   B. Layoffs are increasing
   C. Managers face hiring challenges
   D. Workers stopped job shopping
3. The cultures in today's workforce
   A. More women than men participate in the workforce.
   B. White representation has grown at a slower rate.
   C. Black and Hispanic participation has increased.
   D. Asian participation has decreased.
4. What is true about worker pay?
   A. White men earn the highest pay.
   B. Hispanic women earn more than Hispanic men.
   C. Men earn more than women.
   D. Asian women are the lowest paid.
5. Group experiencing the most discrimination
   A. Asian
   B. Black
   C. Hispanic
   D. White women

CHAPTER 3

Political Actions

Of systems of political power and its impact on the success or demise of companies and communities. Our political representatives and their actions form federal and state policy and legislation combined with corporate board policies and leadership behavior. Actions and decisions from the White House, Congress, and Supreme Court, coupled with responses from corporate board members and company leaders, influence the financial well-being of companies and communities. This chapter offers a snapshot of how politics in the 21st century has created economic disruption in the United States and around the world.

Federal regulations and actions directly influence both the dark and bright sides of the economy, leading to the success or failure of financial institutions. When federal regulations were relaxed in 1999, Bear Stearns, a well-respected financial institution, created highly leveraged and illiquid products before collapsing in 2008. These stocks, bonds, and other instruments are not easily sold or exchanged for cash without a significant loss in value. After this, federal regulations were tightened again to prevent another economic collapse. Board practices sustained JP Morgan during this time. Government policy changes have influenced three economic recessions in the first two decades of the 21st century, with common threads woven through them.

The Dot-Com Recession

The dot-com bubble of the 1990s burst and impacted the U.S. economy between March and December 2001. During this period more than 200 bankruptcies of large businesses were attributed to accounting irregularities, and five of the 10 largest bank failures occurred in 2002.

Leading up to this collapse, in 2000, the Fed and Taxpayer Relief Act reduced interest and tax rates, making debt financing easier. Equity traders rushed to invest in a new industry. The infusion of cash was prompted by the creation of the World Wide Web and growing acceptance of the Internet for online shopping and communication. Compounding the risk were startup companies without business plans and models for running a business, coupled with young entrepreneurs' vision of unimagined wealth and no management experience. The Fed increased interest rates, and the music stopped in March 2000. Nine large businesses failed: Pacific Gas and Electric, Chiquita Brands, Kmart, Enron, Adelphia Communications, Arthur Andersen, WorldCom, Bayou Hedge Fund, and Refco. According to the American Bankruptcy Institute, business bankruptcies reached 40,000 in 2001 and 38,540 in 2022. Gross domestic product (GDP) dropped from 4.82 percent in December 1999 to 1.99 percent December 2002.

The Sarbanes–Oxley Act (SOX), enacted in 2002, required businesses to improve public disclosure. Congress's primary aim was to prevent management from interfering by using an independent audit, to require public companies to ensure accuracy of financial statements, and to make executives responsible for the accuracy and internal control of financial reports.

The Great Recession

The period between December 2007 and June 2009 has been compared to the Great Depression of the 1930s. I remember the day trains stopped delivering cargo to the West Coast. More than eight million jobs were lost and 1.8 million small businesses failed. Several reasons have been attributed to this economic disaster: The Gramm–Leach–Bliley Act of 1999 overturned legislation that prevented banks from combining commercial and investment functions; the Fed lacked the authority to prevent banks from giving mortgages to people who were a bad credit risk; and lax mortgage requirements by the Department of Housing and Urban Development (HUD) directed home mortgages to low-income borrowers, leading to dishonest lending practices. Unregulated investment banks packaged these risky mortgages into mortgage-backed securities and marketed them to their clients. A downturn in the housing market caused these securities to lose value, leading to investment banks losing value and disrupting the economy. Bankruptcies, including Bear Stearns, the Independent National Mortgage Corporation (better known as Indy-Mac), Lehman Brothers, Washington Mutual, and Bernard Madoff, put the brakes on the economy. Business bankruptcies recorded by American Bankruptcy Institute in its "Bankruptcy Statistics" report showed an increase from 28,322 in 2007 to 60,837 in 2009, while GDP fell from 2 percent in 2007 to –2.6 percent in 2009.

The Dodd–Frank Wall Street Reform and Consumer Protection Act was passed in 2010 in response to the bank failures of 2008–2009, with the aim of preventing banks and other financial institutions from becoming "too big to fail." Tests were mandated to ensure large institutions could withstand future financial disruptions and protect consumers from risky financial products. Companies that marketed financial products were regulated. Banks could only trade to run their business or work as an agent, broker, or custodian for their customers. Regulators could identify risks in trades and act before a financial meltdown occurred. Whistleblowers were entitled to as much as 30 percent of the proceeds from successful litigation, and the statute of limitations was extended to 180 days. Hedge funds were required to register with the Securities and Exchange Commission (SEC) and report their trades and portfolios. The insurance industry was monitored to ensure companies followed the law. Access by underserved communities to affordable non-health insurance products was monitored. Bond rating agencies were monitored. Since this disaster, federal regulation has focused on commercial banks, not the investment banks that created the disaster. Some examples of unregulated institutions, also known as shadow banks, include hedge funds, such as Bridgewater and Renaissance Technologies; private equity funds, such as Blackstone and Bain Capital; mortgage lenders, such as Rocket Mortgage, Truist, Chase, and Bank of America; and investment banks, such as JP Morgan Chase, Goldman Sachs, and Bank of America Securities. Investment banks are not regulated because funds originate from investors. Commercial banks are regulated because funds originate from personal checking and saving accounts, loans, and insurance products. The Federal Deposit Insurance Corporation regulates commercial institutions and insures their deposits.

The Pandemic Recession

February to April 2020 was considered the shortest but deepest recession of this century. During this three-month period, federal and state governments shut down the economy in an attempt to stop the spread of the COVID-19 virus. According to the American Bankruptcy Institute, the United States experienced 21,655 business bankruptcies, and GDP shrank to –2.8 percent.

Setting the stage for this economic disaster were two acts by Congress. First, the Tax Cut and Jobs Act (TCJA), passed in December 2017, reduced the corporate tax rate from 35 percent to a 21 percent flat rate. Second, the Economic Growth, Regulatory Relief, and Consumer Protection Act of 2018 reduced the number of banks subject to stronger federal oversight, removed limitations on hedge fund and private equity fund naming conventions, exempted most small banks from the Volcker Rule (part of the Dodd–Frank Wall Street Reform and Consumer Protection Act), reduced regulation, and increased advantages for small- and medium-sized bank holding companies and custodial banks. The act expanded the ability of investment banks to issue closed-ended funds limited to a one-time offer, and offered aid to commercial development entities and municipal obligations. The act was considered by critics to be a massive handout to big banks after corporate tax cuts in 2017.

In their study "The Tax Cuts and Jobs Act: Searching for Supply-Side Effects," William G. Gale and Claire Haldeman of the Brookings Institution and Urban-Brookings Tax Policy Center, July 6, 2021, concluded that the effect was to reduce revenue to the Treasury. "Growth in business formation, employment, and median wages slowed after TCJA was enacted. International profit shifting fell only slightly, and the boost in repatriated profits primarily led to increased share repurchases rather than new investment. Much of the investment increase was concentrated in oil and related industries and appeared to be a response to increases in oil prices, not lower tax rates. Indeed, other investments did not grow very much, and even overall investment growth petered out by the end of 2019."

The $1.2 trillion Infrastructure Investment and Jobs Act was passed in 2021 with bipartisan support. The act's purpose was to rebuild roads and bridges; improve public transit; replace lead pipes and address drinking water contamination; improve high-speed Internet; make port repairs; improve access to clean water; strengthen cybersecurity; and protect infrastructure from weather disasters. Threats of a recession have diminished, unemployment ranges between 3 and 4 percent, and only three major banks have failed including Silicon Valley Bank, Signature Bank, and First Republic Bank. The number of business bankruptcies ranged from 14,347 in 2021 to 18,926 in 2023, while GDP growth ranged from 5.9 percent in 2021 to 2.5 percent in 2023.

In Homer's *Odyssey*, Odysseus warned that

[Circe] said we must avoid the voices of the otherworldly Sirens; steer past their flowering meadow. And she says that I alone should hear their singing. Bind me, to keep me upright at the mast, wound round with rope. If I beseech you and command to set me free, you must increase my bonds and chain even tighter.

Odysseus and other successful leaders resist the songs of the Sirens, which compel them to cut the bonds of regulation and taxation. Those who listen to today's Sirens crash upon rocky shores.

From the stories and data, it is clear that our representatives at the local, state, and federal levels have a major impact on companies and communities. The common thread going through three recessions connects political actions to cut taxes, services, and regulation with business failures. The remedy has been to tighten regulation and increase taxes and services to revive the economy. When the next bubble bursts, the impulse to cut taxes, services, and regulation should be challenged to discern if these actions caused the disruption. Our companies' financial well-being relies on resisting temptations to skirt best practices for fast profits in lieu of responsible tax and regulatory policies for steady economic growth. It goes without saying that how business leaders and managers elect responsible representatives will result in either greater financial stability and growth or another recession.

Five Questions

1. What political actions impact the economy?
   A. Federal regulation
   B. Federal tax policy
   C. FED and agencies
   D. All of the above
2. What caused the Dot-Com Recession?
   A. The Fed and Taxpayer Relief Act
   B. Accounting irregularities
   C. Entrepreneurs with no management experience
   D. All of the above
3. What was not the cause of the Great Recession?
   A. Gramm–Leach–Bliley Act
   B. Dodd–Frank Act
   C. Unregulated investment banks
   D. Dishonest lending practices
4. What did not influence the pandemic recession?
   A. Tax Cut and Jobs Act
   B. Economic Growth Act
   C. Volcker Rule
   D. Economic shutdown
5. Which foundation studied the impact of the Tax Cut and Jobs Act of 2017?
   A. Heritage Foundation
   B. Brookings Institution
   C. American Enterprise Institute
   D. None of the above

CHAPTER 4

Technology Change

How employees are trained and developed to use changing technology matters. How customers are obtained and served with and without technology is becoming critical to the ability of companies to survive or thrive.

Our fourth disruption is technology and its growing impact on companies. How time flies as the pace of changing technology accelerates. Max Roser in his report "Technology Over the Long Run" (February 2023) observes that our ancestors learned to control fire and use it for cooking over 2.4 million years ago. Over the last 12,000 years, agriculture, writing, and the wheel were invented. From 1800, communication advanced from writing on paper to the printing press, telegraph, telephone, radio, the Internet, and smartphones. In 1903, the Wright brothers took the first flight in human history, and just 66 years later we landed on the moon. Technology is changing faster and faster for each generation. The two technology issues affecting companies today include social media and artificial intelligence (AI).

Social Media

Social media refers to technologies that are designed for individuals and organizations to create communities and to communicate ideas, share information, and create content through online interaction. These technologies include platforms such as Facebook, YouTube, Instagram, LinkedIn, WhatsApp, TikTok, WeChat, Messenger, Telegram, Snapchat, Douyin (China's version of TikTok), and Twitter/X. While the benefits are evident, risks abound when using these services in our businesses.

Privacy

Between 2020 and 2024, Meta (owner of Facebook and Instagram, among others) settled lawsuits in Texas, Illinois, and with the Department of Justice (DOJ). The DOJ reached a settlement with Facebook over allegations of discriminatory advertising that violated federal housing law. Lawsuits in Texas and Illinois charged Facebook with illegally using facial recognition technology to collect biometric data from millions of people without their knowledge or permission. Lawsuits have also been filed by parents against Instagram and Facebook, TikTok, Snapchat, X, and YouTube for causing addiction and mental harm to children. School districts are suing social media companies for causing anxiety and depression in students. The 2024 lawsuit involves more than 26 states taking action for allegedly designing addictive features on Instagram, targeting children. So the first threat to our companies and people has to do with these technologies designing systems that directly impact us and our families without our knowledge or permission.

Oversight

The second risk originates from a lack of internal or external oversight and careless messaging. The 2017 Pepsi ad featuring Kendall Jenner handing a police officer a can of Pepsi as a crowd of protesters cheered for peace and love received violent backlash over social media. Many commented it exploited the image of a woman who faced heavily armed police in Baton Rouge, La. during the Black Lives Matter movement. The ad remains a reminder to those relying on social media for advertising.

> Instagram promises parents that its Teen Accounts shield kids from harm "by default." Tests by a Gen Z nonprofit and me—a dad—found it fails spectacularly on some key dimensions.
>
> This spring, Sacramento high school senior Saheb Gulati used a burner phone to create a test Instagram account for a hypothetical 16-year-old boy. As of this past fall, all accounts used by teens are supposed to automatically filter out "sensitive" content, among other protections, for mental health and safety.
>
> Over two weeks, Gulati says, his test account received recommended sexual content that "left very little to the imagination."

He counted at least 28 Instagram Reels describing sexual acts, including digital penetration, using a sex toy and memes describing oral sex. The Instagram account, he says, became preoccupied with "toxic masculinity" discussions about "what men should and shouldn't do."

Four more Gen Z testers, part of a youth organization called Design It for Us, did the same experiment, and all got recommended sexual content. Four of the five got body image and disordered eating content, too, such as a video of a woman saying "skinny is a lifestyle, not a phase."

The young people, whose research was given strategic and operational support by the nonprofit Accountable Tech, also got shown alcohol, drug, hate and other disturbing content. Some are detailed in a report published by Accountable Tech but are too gross to describe here.

A screenshot shows an Instagram video that was recommended to one of the test Teen Accounts. (Washington Post illustration; Accountable Tech via Instagram)

What should be excruciatingly clear to any parent: Instagram's Teen Accounts can't be relied upon to actually shield kids. The danger they face isn't just bad people on the Internet—it's also the app's recommendation algorithm, which decides what your kids see and demonstrates the frightening habit of taking them in dark directions.

For lawmakers weighing a bill to protect kids online, the failures of Instagram's voluntary efforts speak volumes about its accountability.

When I showed the group's report to Instagram's owner, Meta, it said that the youth testers were biased and that some of what they flagged was "unobjectionable" or consistent with "humor from a PG-13 film."

(Column by Geoffrey A. Fowler, *The Washington Post*, May 18, 2025; https://www.washingtonpost.com /technology/2025/05/18/instagram-teen-accounts-test/)

Hacking

LinkedIn was hacked in June 2012, when 165 million users' e-mail and password information was stolen. In 2021 LinkedIn again suffered a breach in which 700 million users' social media information was stolen. Other companies experiencing similar fates include Yahoo in 2013, when 3 billion accounts were exposed, and again in 2014, when 500 million accounts were stolen. Facebook experienced the exposure of 530 million social media accounts, while Marriott International had information stolen from 500 million customers. These data breaches continue to occur. Interviews with Haywood Chamber of Commerce president, CeCe Hipps, and staff members Jean Dilley and Taylor Foxworth reveal the frustration of juggling work while resolving hacks to e-mails, texts, and phones.

Personal Information

In addition to vulnerabilities of hacking, other risks exist. E-mail is frequently used by malware to access data. Engaging links are introduced into devices corrupting software and hardware or stealing data such as financial performance and market strategies.

Clickbait is an engaging headline on social media, enticing readers to click on it only to find misleading information. These clicks lead to websites designed to obtain and use personal information.

Phishing is e-mails using personal information to encourage individuals to click on a link or website where critical information is required such as PINs, passwords, and Social Security numbers. This personal data is used to create fake identities and to access bank accounts. Phishing uses a subject line designed to make the recipient open the e-mail and, in doing so, expose information that can be obtained and used by others. According to research by Jacob Fox reported in the December 2022 edition of Cobalt:

- The most common subject lines for phishing e-mails include words such as urgent, request, important, payment, or attention.
- Only 63 percent of adult respondents to a Proofpoint survey knew what phishing was.

- Ninety percent of all data breaches are linked to phishing attacks, suggesting a need for increased data security.
- Ninety-eight percent of attacks use social engineering.
- Ninety-six percent of all phishing attacks use e-mail as an attack vector, 3 percent come from malicious websites, and 1 percent from phones.
- Phishing is the second most expensive cause of all data breaches.
- LinkedIn phishing messages make up 47 percent of social media phishing attempts, mainly from fake direct messages.

My wife and I sometimes receive e-mails telling us that a relative of our pastor is in distress and needs money. When we check with our pastor, we learn that she has no such relatives. LinkedIn, Instagram, and Facebook seem to be the favorite social media platforms for phishing. In summary, social media is viewed by bad actors as an opportunity to exploit unsuspecting or unprepared companies. Systems are vulnerable to a growing array of threats to our privacy and security.

Artificial Intelligence

It must appear that changes like AI are occurring at the speed of sound. In fact, the birth of AI began toward the end of World War II when a brilliant British mathematician named Alan Turing proposed that machines could learn, and then built the prototype for today's computers. His idea was that learning machines could perform the tasks usually done by humans. The ability of a machine or robot to do such tasks is now referred to as AI. Dartmouth College pioneered research on AI in 1956 with funding by the U.S. Department of Defense. During the first decade of the 21st century, Google developed more than 2,700 AI-related projects, leading to the introduction of OpenAI's writing and learning program ChatGPT on November 30, 2022. From the time of Turing to today, more than 70 years have elapsed in the development of this "new technology."

Chaos has reigned since the introduction of ChatGPT by OpenAI, the darling of big tech and U.S. hedge fund investors. The company's founder, Sam Altman, and board members including Elon Musk, intended for OpenAI to serve the public good as a nonprofit offering open-source AI systems. As demand for services grew, pressure increased to transform the nonprofit into a publicly traded company to grow the enterprise. On its website, they comment, "We are excited to introduce ChatGPT to get users' feedback and learn about its strengths and weaknesses. During the research preview, usage of ChatGPT is free. Try it now at chat.openai.com."

For most of its existence, Big Tech has practiced an engineering concept referred to as "rapid spiral development." Product development is based on the quick build and release of products rather than beta testing before release. Beta testing is a process in which select clients use and attempt to break the product until its flaws have been worked out. The goal of rapid spiral development is to quickly capture market share using unsuspecting customers to provide feedback on defects. For example, Tesla released self-driving cars resulting in serious accidents and deaths. Space X blew up four rockets before achieving a successful launch. Microsoft typically had bugs in each of its Office software releases that were patched when enough users complained. Microsoft recently introduced its AI program Copilot. When customers complained that the system had problems and was not as good as ChatGPT, they were blamed for failing to use Copilot properly.

Apple announced that it was integrating ChatGPT across its operating systems and apps. Siri will be able to connect with ChatGPT to find answers to questions. As excitement grows with these greater efficiencies, along with enhanced customer service, it becomes critical to take a thoughtful approach to new resources for collaboration.

It is understandable why society is anxious and reluctant to participate in this brave new world. I surveyed nearly 600 subscribers of my weekly blog. I asked, "What do you want to know about AI?" Responses included being able to distinguish between fact and fiction, keeping up with changes, how to safely use the technology, what control limits are installed to create content and give advice, and how consumers will know if information is from reliable sources. Participants were then asked: "What concerns you about AI?" Answers included concerns about the validity of information derived from AI, job losses to robots, AI control of society as we become dependent on its resources, and changes in how we think and create content. I concluded that much is to be gained by educating the public in open access forums regarding their concerns and facts as we know them. As noted in a BBC News article by Zoe Kleinman and Chris Vallance (May 2, 2023), AI's "godfather" Geoffrey Hinton warns of dangers as he quits Google. The article highlights concerns about the future of AI. They reported that Dr. Geoffrey Hinton, 75, retired from Google with regrets. Referred to as the "godfather of AI," he shared his concerns about chatbots with the reporters saying, "Right now, they're not more intelligent than us, as far as I can tell. But I think they soon may be." He explained that bots possess greater information capacity than people saying, "Right now, what we're seeing is things like GPT-4 eclipses a person in the amount of general knowledge it has and it eclipses them by a long way. In terms of reasoning, it is not as good, but it does already do simple reasoning," he said. "And given the rate of progress, we expect things to get better quite fast. So we need to worry about that." His concern is that AI will gain greater learning capacity than humans and be used for misguided purposes. Evidently many others agree with Dr. Hinton.

The Future of Life Institute published an open letter titled "Pause Giant AI Experiments: An Open Letter" (22 March, 2023). It received more than 30,000 signatures, including academic AI researchers and industry CEOs such as Yoshua Bengio, Stuart Russell, Elon Musk, Steve Wozniak, and Yuval Noah Harari.[2] The full content is below:

We call on all AI labs to immediately pause for at least 6 months the training of AI systems more powerful than GPT-4.

AI systems with human-competitive intelligence can pose profound risks to society and humanity, as shown by extensive research and acknowledged by top AI labs. As stated in the widely-endorsed Asilomar AI Principles, *Advanced AI could represent a profound change in the history of life on Earth, and should be planned for and managed with commensurate care and resources.* Unfortunately, this level of planning and management is not happening, even though recent months have seen AI labs locked in an out-of-control race to develop and deploy ever more powerful digital minds that no one—not even their creators—can understand, predict, or reliably control.

---

[2]https://en.wikipedia.org/wiki/Pause_Giant_AI_Experiments:_An_Open_Letter

Contemporary AI systems are now becoming human-competitive at general tasks, and we must ask ourselves: *Should* we let machines flood our information channels with propaganda and untruth? *Should* we automate away all the jobs, including the fulfilling ones? *Should* we develop nonhuman minds that might eventually outnumber, outsmart, obsolete and replace us? *Should* we risk loss of control of our civilization? Such decisions must not be delegated to unelected tech leaders. Powerful AI systems should be developed only once we are confident that their effects will be positive and their risks will be manageable. This confidence must be well justified and increase with the magnitude of a system's potential effects. OpenAI's recent statement regarding artificial general intelligence, states that *"At some point, it may be important to get independent review before starting to train future systems, and for the most advanced efforts to agree to limit the rate of growth of compute used for creating new models."* We agree. That point is now.

Therefore, **we call on all AI labs to immediately pause for at least 6 months the training of AI systems more powerful than GPT-4.** This pause should be public and verifiable, and include all key actors. If such a pause cannot be enacted quickly, governments should step in and institute a moratorium.

AI labs and independent experts should use this pause to jointly develop and implement a set of shared safety protocols for advanced AI design and development that are rigorously audited and overseen by independent outside experts. These protocols should ensure that systems adhering to them are safe beyond a reasonable doubt. This does *not* mean a pause on AI development in general, merely a stepping back from the dangerous race to ever-larger unpredictable black-box models with emergent capabilities.

AI research and development should be refocused on making today's powerful, state-of-the-art systems more accurate, safe, interpretable, transparent, robust, aligned, trustworthy, and loyal.

In parallel, AI developers must work with policy makers to dramatically accelerate development of robust AI governance systems. These should at a minimum include: new and capable regulatory authorities dedicated to AI; oversight and tracking of highly capable AI systems and large pools of computational capability; provenance and watermarking systems to help distinguish real from synthetic and to track model leaks; a robust auditing and certification ecosystem; liability for AI-caused harm; robust public funding for technical AI safety research; and well-resourced institutions for coping with the dramatic economic and political disruptions (especially to democracy) that AI will cause.

Humanity can enjoy a flourishing future with AI. Having succeeded in creating powerful AI systems, we can now enjoy an "AI summer" in which we reap the rewards, engineer these systems for the clear benefit of all, and give society a chance to adapt. Society has hit pause on other technologies with potentially catastrophic effects on society. We can do so here. Let's enjoy a long AI summer, not rush unprepared into a fall.

(https://futureoflife.org/open-letter/pause-giant-ai
-experiments/; emphasis in original)

The letter received praise and criticism and of this writing very little action has been taken. In the meantime, it may be helpful to consider the disruptions we experience from both social media and AI.

Trust

Have you ever wondered if the person on the other end of the phone is human? Occasionally, I feel a need to ask those answering my call or online chat, "Are you a human?" Those who are, laugh. Nonhumans disconnect my call. From the early days of software development, trust issues have existed. Early in my career, I was a human resource deputy for a software company. I will never forget the day our product development officer notified me he terminated his project manager because she told the truth in a client meeting.

In the article "How enterprise capabilities influence customer trust and behavior?" in *Deloitte Insights Magazine*, Michael Bondar, Roxana

Corduneanu, Natasha Buckley, and David Levin (June 28, 2022) offer insights into trust and technology:

> Overall trust in the technology sector has fallen in the United States, as the sector moved from first place among the most trusted sectors in 2020 to ninth in 2021.[1] Recent studies indicate that many tech customers, both end users and business-to-business (B2B) purchasers, lack trust in the organizations from which they purchase. In a fall 2021 survey, almost three out of four B2B purchasers surveyed said that "tech vendors typically fall short of being honest."[2] This lack of trust can make it challenging for technology brands to drive growth and achieve their mission and purpose.

The uncertainty created by inaccurate information was emphasized by John and Richard, two technical advisers who help people with their technology questions. "We used to rely on our critical thinking," said John, "but now there is too much information coming at us that is not true or accurate. I had trouble ordering from Amazon. I am asked to set up an account and all I want is to buy a chainsaw chain. I do not want an account with Amazon. AI was used to communicate with me after forcing me to make choices on what I need help with. The bot sends me somewhere else and does not answer my question. I committed to stop using Amazon for online orders. Who do we trust?"

Financial Pressure

Pressure comes with public offerings. Quarterly reports on stock performance become an obsession, creating unrealistic milestones for product development and release. Additionally, competition is a constant threat to financial well-being. How long before a product is reverse engineered, or an employee leaves to produce a better version? As a result of such pressures, products are released before they are fully tested. Eric Ries, an American entrepreneur, author, and speaker popularized the "lean startup" methodology, focusing on rapid experimentation, customer feedback, and iterative development. He defined minimum viable product (MVP) as that version of a new product that allows a team to collect the maximum amount of validated learning about customers with the least effort. A key premise is that a product is produced and offered to customers before adequate testing. Observing and learning what people do with a product is much more reliable than asking them what they would do. Consumers participate in final testing as they wrestle with bugs and system errors. The software company for whom I worked used beta testing on every product prior to release. Our beta clients tested and attempted to break our systems. Only after complete testing would our products be introduced to the market. This process has been replaced with less deliberate testing in the rush to capture market share, regardless of costly repairs, harm to customers, and potential litigation.

Learning Curve

Employees may just be getting comfortable with existing systems when they are asked to learn a new system or a product enhancement. Extended training time for additional learning may be daunting. Increasingly heavy workloads are why more than 60 percent of employees do not believe they have an opportunity to learn during working hours. A lack of quality training compounds the problem. During one interview, I heard complaints about vendor training missing the mark. It appears that PowerPoint presentations and lectures amplify learning challenges.

Generations and Cultures

In a workshop I conducted on changing workplaces, participants agreed that age differences create challenges in adapting to new and improved technology. Millennials and Gen Z are easier to train than baby boomers and Gen X according to John and Richard, our technical advisers. Older people may skip upgrades on their devices and experience difficulties adapting to new systems. Cultural differences also create challenges. John observed that he and some of his Latinx clients experienced communication glitches because of their limited English and his limited Spanish language skills.

Customer Experience

We have heard about the great things AI will do to enhance customer experiences. An online search provides multiple pages of business articles and marketing materials on exceptional customer experiences using new systems. I have to wonder whether any of these proponents have made a phone call for help with a vacuum cleaner, insurance claim, or pickup truck repair.

One of the greatest risks to business growth is reliance on technology for customer communication. Customers seek a personal connection when learning about new products, solving problems, and gaining knowledge. AI's ability to mimic human behavior has advanced, but most consumers know the difference between a human and an automated system's limited options. The transformation to technology for customer connections and communication builds barriers between companies and consumers. Have you experienced making a call and being directed by a voice to press 1, 2, 3, or 4? The voice/machine does not understand, so you repeat the process before giving your information. Then you get a voice that sounds human and, sure enough, you are finally talking to a person who asks for the same information. The person is unable to help and you get transferred to someone on another continent, where English is a second language. "People are having difficulty having what I would describe as an authentic interaction," said Scott Broetzmann with Customer Care Measurement and Consulting. "Technology, for all of its benefits that it affords us, when it comes to having a problem and trying to get it resolved, in many cases it serves as an impediment," Broetzmann said. According to ANA Marketing (January 16, 2025), "The 2025 National Customer Rage Survey reveals an all-time high in customer problem experiences at 74 percent, with nearly $888 billion in revenue at risk due to ineffective complaint handling and growing customer incivility."

Regulation

The lack of government oversight and consequences for bad behavior are concerning, as legislators create self-regulating legislation that allows big tech to correct its own behavior. According to *Politico* on September 21,

2023, "Senate Minority Whip John Thune (Republican, South Dakota) is teaming up with Senator Amy Klobuchar (Democrat, Minnesota) on legislation that would require companies to assess the impact of AI systems and self-certify the safety of systems seen as particularly risky." So much for regulation. The representatives we choose determine policies for how we live our lives and run our businesses but Big Tech has free reign. Strong representatives are required if we are to have regulation of Big Tech.

In summary, it has become easy to accept things as they happen and justify inaction because it is technology and we are helpless to do anything at all. We are allowing Big Tech to pave the road for us to travel in our electric vehicles straight to their banks. Political action and inaction have proven to be no solution at all. Our legislators have been influenced by Big Tech who feed their mantra of free enterprise to our representatives as they go through the motions of helping us with nothing to show for it other than generous donations. More than 30,000 signatures on a warning letter had little to no impact. I have learned the combination of political actions and technology is central to the turbulence we are experiencing. How we respond to our political representatives matters if we expect to see changes for the better for our communities and companies.

Five Questions

1. Which of the following is not a social media platform?
   A. Telegram
   B. Instagram
   C. ChatGPT
   D. TikTok
2. Which of these social media facts are not true?
   A. Ninety percent of all data breaches are phishing attacks.
   B. Ninety-six percent of all phishing attacks use e-mail.
   C. Phishing is the least expensive cause of data breaches.
   D. LinkedIn phishing messages make up 47 percent of social media phishing.

3. Which of these descriptions do not apply to social media?
   A. Discriminatory advertising
   B. Illegal use of facial recognition systems
   C. Quality child education
   D. Mental harm to children
4. Which of the following AI risks can disrupt companies?
   A. Trust
   B. Lack of regulation
   C. Poor customer experience
   D. All of the above
5. The Open Letter by the Future of Life Institute does not recommend:
   A. Regulatory authorities
   B. Deregulation of AI
   C. Oversight and tracking of AI
   D. Watermarking

Answers, Disruption

Chapter 1   1 = B; 2 = C; 3 = C; 4 = D; 5 = D
Chapter 2   1 = C; 2 = D 3 = B+D; 4 = C; 5 = B
Chapter 3   1 = D; 2 = D; 3 = B; 4 = C; 5 = B
Chapter 4   1 = C; 2 = C; 3 = C; 4 = D; 5 = B

PART 2

Strategy

Whether and how we plan matters. The causes of survival and growth come from charting a system of assumptions and facts that enable a community and company to continually innovate and succeed, no matter what eruptions may occur. Failure to plan, execute the plan, review the impact of actions taken, and revise plans is a prescription for failure in today's turbulence and uncertainty.

CHAPTER 5

Study

Achieving resilience involves disciplined planning. A woven growth strategy includes assumptions made when responding to the headwinds of climate disasters, social change, political actions, and technology change. Let's consider strategies that strengthen the components of our companies and take lessons from the actions of others. Today's strategic planning process includes four steps (Figure 5.1).

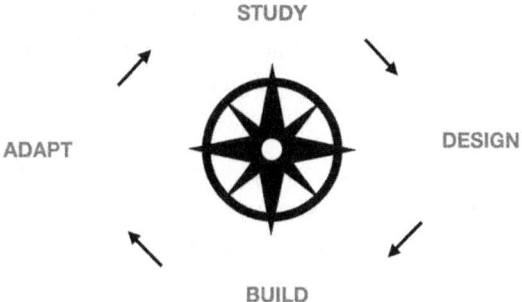

Figure 5.1 Four-Step Business Model

Four-Step Business Model

1. *Study* the ecosystem to determine the status of competitors, suppliers, and internal culture.
2. *Design* a strategy for moving forward using assumptions anticipating risks of disruption.
3. *Build* the company through strategy implementation.
4. *Adapt* to changing circumstances by regular and frequent strategy reviews and modification. The process clarifies how board and management team's expectations for growth guide decisions for designing and building resilient organizations.

Three Horizons for Growth

Mehrdad Baghai, Stephen Coley, and David White, principals with the consulting firm McKinsey & Company, in their book *The Alchemy of Growth* presented a growth model based on observations of companies they serve. They call their model "Three Horizons."

The purpose of their three horizons model is to assist leaders consider their options for incremental or disruptive growth. Originally companies would choose one of three options. However, the model evolved into an understanding that all three horizons can be included in a total growth strategy rather than one horizon. Leaders have choices in how disruptive they wish to be by choosing one or all options.

Horizon 1: Improve. This represents continually improving processes, products, and services. For example, Volvo built its first vehicle in 1927 in Gothenburg, Sweden. It grew its base of vehicles using the principles of continuous improvement. They advanced to Innovate status. In 1996, Flash Engineering (later renamed Polestar Racing), a Swedish motorsport team, used Volvo models to win more than a hundred European races.

Horizon 2: Expand. This encompasses emerging opportunities, including those ventures likely to generate substantial profits and expansion to new customers and markets. In 1944, Volvo expanded into international markets and by 1974 the United States had become its largest market.

Horizon 3: Innovate. This horizon contains ideas for disrupting markets for competitive advantage or for countering emerging threats. In 2000, Volvo was sold to Ford Motor Company and in 2010 to Chinese automaker, Geely. In 2015, Volvo acquired Polestar Racing and fully integrated both operations by 2017 with a mission to produce only electric vehicles. The Polestar 2 was introduced in 2019 followed by the Polestar 3 SUV, then the Polestar 4 SUV coupe, with more on the horizon. The company's goal is to become climate neutral by 2030. In the case of Volvo and Polestar, the three horizons occurred sequentially over many years. However, there are innovation-driven companies in which the time frames for horizon options are condensed from years to months.

How Two Organizations Practiced Study

McDonald's DC region serves as an example for combining all three horizons into one strategy. Teams of managers and crew members drove through competitors' parking lots at noon, counting cars to determine market share. They ordered drive-through meals and timed order fulfillment. They sampled the food and evaluated the accuracy, taste, and temperature of each meal. After studying their competition, they evaluated their own restaurants using the same criteria (number of cars in parking lots, speed of service, and food quality). This comparative data was used to design and build a strategy for gaining market share.

I used these concepts to turn around a nonprofit—Circles of Hope. My first step was to collect data on its financial status. The second step was interviewing program volunteers, and the third step was surveying community stakeholders and former volunteers. The survey asked: "What would you start doing, stop doing, and continue doing?" The results showed the following:

- A bank account with $20,000
- A list of 200 volunteers, with an active volunteer count of 15
- Volunteers were exhausted; they volunteered to perform one duty but were asked to do much more.
- Volunteers possessed valuable competencies and passions
- Volunteer turnover generated by disorganization within the program
- A program that was viewed by community members as being of value but disorganized

This data made it clear that certain actions were necessary before we could create a growth strategy. The first step was to organize our volunteers into work groups with responsibility for each component of the organization: finance, operations, volunteers, and clients. People were assigned to groups based on their skills and passion. Frustration evaporated as workloads were simplified and members used their skills to make a difference in the lives of people working their way out of poverty. This effort was part of my effort to change the culture of the program.

There are two considerations regarding studying culture. The first has to do with management behavior and the second concerns the spirit of integrity that permeates the atmosphere of an enterprise.

1. Management Behavior

These provide a snapshot of leadership influence on workforce behavior. There are five talents that influence company performance and culture.

- Talent 1. Workforce is aligned with strategy. This refers to how managers involve their people in developing and implementing company plans.
- Talent 2. Communication and response to change. The manner in which managers listen before speaking and engage employees in change initiatives has a positive impact on people and productivity.
- Talent 3. Decision making and problem solving. When employees participate in making decisions affecting them and solve work-related problems together, it increases efficiency and reduces costs.
- Talent 4. Motivation within the workforce. Companies with managers who see their people doing something good and who celebrate improvements and goal achievement have happy employees.
- Talent 5. Quality and quantity of innovation within the workplace. When creativity and innovation are encouraged, companies become healthier.

Over several years I noticed a pattern in survey responses: The Communication and Motivation score was significantly higher than Workforce Alignment, Decision Making and Problem Solving, and Quality and Quantity scores. When all five management talents are applied consistently, companies create cultures of resilience.

2. Integrity

Integrity reflects how company boards and leadership teams balance the pursuit of wealth with an adherence to principles. Facebook's involvement in fake news and clandestine marketing to children, prompted an attorney to comment about the unbridled pursuit of wealth in some companies today.

I developed an integrity index to gauge workplace perceptions of their company's emphasis on wealth versus concern with principles. The index has been used to validate assumptions when designing today's strategies. Four options describe the choices boards and leadership teams make for their companies.

1. Amoral: Low Principles and High Wealth. The focus is on wealth creation and conveys the message that the end justifies the means. Wells Fargo was fined for mandating that each unit generate specified amounts of client fees and was convicted of red-lining minority neighborhoods.

2. Nomad: Low Principles and Low Wealth. Leadership lacks focus and communicates conflicting expectations to associates and stakeholders. A nonprofit was successful in creating and passing legislation for cleaner air. Afterward it drifted and began participating in other endeavors with less relevance to clean air initiatives. It lost support and ultimately failed.

3. Principled: High Principles and Low Wealth. The leadership focus is about doing good work and achieving respect within the organization and community. As Sam Altman of OpenAI learned, devotion to principles can distract from the financial well-being of the organization. Over time he has transitioned OpenAI into a hybrid model, in which a nonprofit and for-profit organization are combined to balance principles and pursue wealth. There is continual stress between holding to its values and generating greater profits.

4. Balanced: High Principles and High Wealth. The focus takes a balanced approach to conducting business. Clearly stated principles are evident and staff can describe how each principle is practiced. Everyone knows the organization's financial status and works to enhance its well-being. These organizations become stronger and are more sustainable during threatening periods. Chick fil-A is an example of a balanced approach. No matter how many times the owners are encouraged to open restaurants on Sundays, they refuse. The company continues to grow financially as it lives by its principles.

Culture surveys and integrity indexes are examples of survey instruments offering insight into the culture of companies and nonprofits. Other instruments including focus groups and online surveys are also generating culture data. No matter how data are derived, it is important to clearly define the existing culture when developing strategies for strengthening companies for today's chaos and confusion.

Five Questions

1. Which two steps are part of the four-step business model?
   A. Assess
   B. Design
   C. Build
   D. Evaluate
2. Which step is not included in the Three Horizons?
   A. Renovate
   B. Expand
   C. Innovate
   D. Improve
3. Culture includes
   A. Management behavior
   B. Problem solving
   C. All of the above
   D. None the above
4. Which option bankrupted two organizations?
   A. Low principles–high wealth
   B. High principles–low wealth
   C. High principles–high wealth
   D. Low principles–low wealth
5. What did McDonald's study?
   A. Car counts
   B. Menu choices
   C. Service speed
   D. All of the above

CHAPTER 6

Design

Design involves processing information obtained in the study stage through the lens of past, present, and future events. Including stakeholders such as employees, management, suppliers, investors, and customers creates opportunities for resolving long-standing problems that have restrained companies from becoming resilient. Design includes a reflection on the four repetitive disruptions over the past 10 years and the present. That information creates the springboard for making informed assumptions for future growth and resilience. For example, climate disasters over the past 10 years have impacted business successes and failures. Society's growing complexity, including a diminishing supply of labor and an increasingly diverse population, influences how we recruit and retain employees and customers. Politics at the federal and state level impose policies that dramatically impact our financial stability including three recessions in this century. Technology, with a total lack of meaningful regulation, impacts company financials, operations, workforce, and clients. Identifying how each of these disruptors affect our companies provides valuable insights for defining goals and tactics to build resiliency and sustainability within organizations and communities. One of my clients was an insurance company in which financial data were the only information available. This client considered strategic planning to be setting challenging sales goals for its agents and staff. They, like others who focus solely on financials, may gain greater income, but the core of their company's operations can become obsolete, employee spirit diminishes, and the company's perspective shifts, viewing customers as price points rather than human beings. Those who want to broaden their strategies focus on operational goals for efficiency, new or improved equipment and technology; those considering their financial goals target both increased income and reduced costs; those focusing on their workforce goals focus on enhancing performance, reducing employee turnover, enhancing skill sets, and recruiting new personnel; those aiming to broaden their customer goals focus on increasing the number of customers, analyzing customers' purchasing habits, and increasing satisfaction with company communication and services.

Corporate Design

Unlike the insurance client, when serving McDonald's Washington, DC Region, the people invited to the strategy sessions included stakeholders such as "the bread man" (the bun supplier) and other suppliers, accountants, human resources personnel, corporate marketing, restaurant crew members and managers, and profit center directors. It was not possible to include all 3,000 employees, so we invited representatives from each profit center. Across the walls of the boardroom were flip chart pages labeled for the four components of their business. These charts were used for brainstorming and problem solving. The directors presented competitor and company analysis. They took questions for as long as people needed answers. Then planning began. Everyone chose a station and had seven minutes to brainstorm ideas for making their component stronger. They rotated clockwise to add ideas to each station. Once brainstorming was complete each group selected a spokesperson to present their ideas to the whole group.

After a break, decision making began. Everyone voted on the top four items that could most impact their business. We finished when everyone agreed on actions for each component. The final step was action planning. Everyone identified goals and tasks for their station. They knew they were through when everyone agreed on actions for their region to gain market share. They were all smiles. Dave Natysin moved around the room shaking hands and patting backs before offering final thoughts. I do not remember a word he said, but I still get tight inside as I remember all those people proudly smiling. It had been quite a day!

My fondest memories of that experience were William Williams who played high school basketball against Phil Ford, the all-American point guard for University of North Carolina (UNC). He was watching as I tried to hang a flip chart page high on the wall. "Hell, Robinson," he yelled. "You know white men can't jump!" William got the honor of hanging our flip chart pages high on the wall.

The results of that strategy event were monumental. The team accepted the challenges of all three horizons:

- Horizon 1: Make continuous improvements in restaurant operations and customer satisfaction.
- Horizon 2: Expand the market by building 30 restaurants.
- Horizon 3: Innovate a new restaurant model.

Nonprofit Design

The lessons from McDonald's were on my mind when planning a retreat for the nonprofit, Circles of Hope. I realized that aligning everyone in the organization with our plans was critical to our survival and achieving resilience.

Our volunteers agreed on a time to gather; county commissioners, nonprofit directors, and other community stakeholders accepted the invitation. For the event we ran a long stretch of paper across the wall in our church meeting room. As guests arrived and mingled, they acknowledged one another with cautious smiles. For the most part, I noticed them keeping to themselves and avoiding contact with others. It was eerily quiet, no laughter. I was not worried. I knew these people and believed they would give this experience a chance. As I described the process of evaluating our experiences in the past and present to plan for the future, I could see friendly looks in the group. I felt better.

Morning Session

The morning gradually gained momentum as people moved to the long chart on the wall and engaged in reflection on the impact of past and present on our nonprofit. When we stopped for lunch, we found the results to be incredibly revealing. Here is what we discovered (Table 6.1).

- Climate. Our mountain community was located in a valley. That location made building difficult anywhere other than limited space in the valley.

Table 6.1 Analysis

Disruption	Past 10 years	Present day	Future assumptions
Climate	Slowly changing	Since 2020 disruptions are more frequent and intense	Increasingly extreme climate disasters
Social	Limited diversity and ample labor supply	Greater diversity, limited labor, and immigration issues	Resolution of immigration issues lead to a labor surplus with greater diversity
Politics	Two changes impact downturns in the economy	Stable economy	More stability or instability
Technology	Social media evolution	Artificial intelligence	Robots take over the world

- Social. We learned that poorer people remain in poverty because they are under pressure to have an income and work, so they find low-paying jobs to get by. We should find living wage jobs. We realized affordable housing was limited. We should establish relationships with local landlords.
- Politics. We realized that influential government officials tend to blame the victims for their dire situations. Some officials assumed people chose to be poor and live on welfare. To appeal for their financial support, we agreed to communicate how the nonprofit's services save county and state dollars by lifting people out of poverty and out of a reliance on government services. This appealed to their instincts. We also considered adding business owners and community leaders to the organization's board (Table 6.2).
- Technology. This was an eye-opener. We tracked the evolution of computers from mainframes to phones and realized that society relies on smartphones. However, our clients could not afford such phones and used prepaid ones instead. They experienced frustration when communicating with potential employers. They needed smartphones to obtain living wage jobs.

Table 6.2 Response to disruption

Disruptors	Finance	Operations	Volunteers	Clients
Climate		Petition for more public transportation		Create Landlord relationships
Social	Luncheons Grants	Group meetings to evaluate ways to improve	Design and implement volunteer recognition programs	Business survey of living wage jobs by Western Carolina University
Politics	Invite county commissioners to activities	Present success stories to county commissioners		Improve client training Start financial training
Technology	iPads and iPhones	Install training on iPads		Train clients to use iPads and iPhones

Afternoon Session

In the afternoon, we built a growth strategy for each part of the organization. The strategy was designed using the data from the morning study session. I felt goose bumps hearing people whispering and laughing as they wrote their ideas on the chart. Here is their strategy.

- Finance. Set goals to raise money for smartphones and iPads. We made plans to sustain the program through donations, county grants, and annual luncheons.
- Operations. We made plans to investigate installing course materials onto iPads for clients to use in training. We also agreed on steps to improve client training experiences using a team approach.
- Employees. We made plans to improve recognition of volunteers. We scheduled times and events to celebrate the tireless work they contribute.
- Clients. We agreed to focus on landlord relationships for housing opportunities, increase training topics such as financial management, and focus job searches on companies that paid

a living wage. We would recruit Western Carolina University social work students to conduct a survey of businesses in our community to learn local pay practices and target companies paying a living wage.

We completed our work late in the day, with everyone choosing tasks and completion dates for the action plan. There were broad smiles all around as we reached final agreement. The participants' demeanor changed over the course of the day. Several people shared business cards, and others agreed to meet later to help each other with their issues. Two directors, who had refused to speak to each other in the morning, left together giggling. My smile was just as big as theirs.

Five Questions

1. Designing a plan does not include:
    A. Stakeholders
    B. Five disruptions
    C. Four components
    D. Past, present, future
2. Steps in the design phase of planning include:
    A. Presenting the study findings
    B. Brainstorming ideas and solutions
    C. Everyone agrees
    D. All of the above
3. The four components do not include:
    A. Stakeholders
    B. Financials
    C. Employees
    D. Customers
4. Disruptive forces do not include:
    A. Politics
    B. Economy
    C. Climate
    D. Technology

5. What McDonald's and Circles of Hope had in common?
   A. A variety of stakeholders participated
   B. Focus was strengths and weaknesses
   C. Focus was threats and opportunities
   D. All of the above

CHAPTER 7

Build

Imagine devoting an extreme amount of time, energy, and money when creating an innovative strategy, only for it to gather dust on a shelf until the next planning session a year or two later. The leader of a local community college observed that the inability to execute plans and strategies is a key obstacle to business success. He observed that the secret to a thriving business lies in successful implementation of its strategy. Build is the stage for implementing tactics and achieving goals. It puts life into a strategy. The Action Plan is the secret ingredient for companies and communities to implement strategic planning.

Action Plans

When using an action plan, participants write their commitments in the *what* section and their names in the *who* section. Target dates for completion are entered in the *when* section. Teams review their action plans either weekly or monthly and the status of each item is recorded during these accountability meetings. Here is an example (Table 7.1).

This tool was incredibly helpful for weekly and monthly reviews with volunteers in the Circles of Hope program. Each of the teams met either weekly or monthly, depending on their projects. Each team reviewed the goals and tasks developed during our strategy retreat. For example, the finance team met monthly to review each member's achievements raising funds. Throughout the month, members met as frequently as weekly to coordinate their

Table 7.1 Action plan to implement plans and strategies

What	Who	When	Status
Evaluate AI for improving operational processes	Lea	February 3, 2024	
Order iPads	Tony	August 15, 2023	Done

activities. For example, those who were writing grants met monthly; those responsible for fundraisers and the annual luncheon met weekly.

My job was to provide information and resources. Occasionally, I would facilitate if the meeting got sticky. For example, if conversations went off topic, I would remind attendees of their topic and gently lead them back to their original discussion, for example, "I'm confused. Weren't we talking about handouts for our fundraiser? How did we get on to Jack's new truck?" Most of the time they laughed and thanked me. There were a few occasions, however, when it would have been better if I sat quietly, according to the elementary school teacher who led the group. I learned that should I ever need help, find an elementary school teacher. Mostly, I was a cheerleader, celebrating small and huge successes.

Our board met monthly and a representative from each group attended with a progress update. Sometimes several team members would attend to add to the discussions and receive recognition for their contributions. The board was great at reviewing plans, providing resources, and offering encouragement. It was key to the program's growth, which improved to $100,000, and to increasing productivity to two graduating cohorts per year. They executed the complete strategy.

Other Tools

Implementing a strategy moves a company forward at a faster clip and with greater efficiency than simply posting mission and vision statements on a wall. Having reports of successful implementation increases momentum for taking additional steps forward. When constructing McDonald's restaurants around Washington, DC, we began getting excited when several buildings began rising at the same time. When landlords began attending our Circles of Hope meetings, we began to get excited about more affordable housing for our clients. It is worth staying focused and being patient to see progress and inform everyone as that happens.

Organize Teams with Strategy

Teams should be aligned with the strategic plan. McDonald's organized people around its strategy and scorecard. Both hourly crew members and managers from each profit center were part of each strategy team. The financial management group consisted of operations personnel along with human resources and accounting staff members. The operations group consisted of operations, engineering, real estate, accounting, and human resources personnel. The customer satisfaction team consisted of operations, marketing, sales, real estate, and accounting staff. Finally, the employee satisfaction group had representatives from operations, human resources, and accounting. These groups met monthly to review goals and develop action plans for the coming month. Graphs were updated in these meetings.

Circles of Hope was a much smaller enterprise and had a simpler organizational structure for strategy implementation. I organized everyone who had participated in the planning session into four teams who developed goals and action plans. During the year every team meeting focused on completing action plans developed in the retreat. Just as McDonald's, Circles of Hope succeeded in growing and thriving in their community.

Track Progress

Daily operations can easily overshadow plans made at the beginning of the year. Managers can overlook their strategic role as they work to accomplish their daily responsibilities. So making work fun is part of achieving strategies and goals. For example, I obsess over UNC basketball because I watch game scores, win/loss records, and national rankings. Similarly, tracking key performance indicators (KPIs) allows organizations to identify and solve problems early, adapt, and remain on track. The coach and players on sports teams know immediately if they are winning or losing. I know after each play how well UNC is competing. Data tracking tools are invaluable for having a clear picture of the business and for making informed decisions. As an example, monitoring such data has become an obsession for many who participate in sports betting. For your business, if there is an operations objective to reduce waste from 15 to 10 percent of total materials produced, managers know to continue their procedures by monitoring data. However, should the chart report waste increasing to 20 percent, managers know to adjust their process and monitor closely. For larger operations this KPI might be part of a balanced scorecard or dashboard to track implementation of strategic tactics. On the McDonald's project, graphs were posted in the boardroom for employees, managers, suppliers, and guests to witness progress. Many visitors were impressed by this management team's transparency with its numbers. The workforce was proud to tell anyone and everyone about its actions to make their numbers and achieve their goals on their balanced scorecards.

McDonald's KPIs were monitored weekly at the regional level, in all six profit centers, and at every restaurant. Each restaurant employed approximately 60 people, and a profit center comprised between six and 10 restaurants. The regional KPIs tracked sales and costs; profit center KPIs measured utility, labor, and food costs and sales; and each restaurant measured outcomes such as attendance, food waste, customer satisfaction, drive-through times, order accuracy, and sales. I attended these meetings to advise and coach on meeting facilitation, problem solving, group decision making, as well as employee and customer satisfaction issues.

Workforce Commitment

Rather than introducing their new strategy to everyone and asking for support, leaders could do more to motivate and engage employees. For traditionally run companies, telling a story explaining the strategy's relevance and potential market impact is an improvement. We see this at the annual shows conducted by big tech leaders as they announce new products and strategies to their associates and the world.

More enlightened organizations gain commitment and ownership by involving employees in the development and execution of strategic initiatives. Leaders inspire support when employees have a say in creating and implementing the strategy. Regular updates and open forums keep everyone informed and engaged. Motivation happens when leaders regularly meet with employee groups, offer progress updates, ask for and use employees' ideas, and recognize those people moving the strategy forward. This is critical to growing and competing over the coming years of uncertainty.

Five Questions

1. Action plans include:
   A. What
   B. Who
   C. How
   D. Where
2. Strategy implementation includes:
   A. Organizing teams with strategy
   B. Tracking progress
   C. Both
   D. Neither
3. The role of the leader in strategy meetings includes:
   A. Keep humor and good will in the team
   B. Provide information and resources
   C. Facilitate meetings
   D. Keep discussions on track
4. KPI means:
   A. Keep Process Integrity
   B. Key Performance Indicator
   C. Keep People Informed
   D. All of the above
5. Gaining workforce commitment for strategic goals includes:
   A. Informing workers of management decisions
   B. Including workers in decisions
   C. Asking workers for their support
   D. All of the above

CHAPTER 8

Adapt

Adapt involves anticipating and reacting to unforeseen changes such as Hurricane Helene and record-breaking wildfires in California; political shifts in ideology; social issues such as fewer people available to work, disruptions like COVID-19 pandemic, and changing norms; and evolving technology such as social media developments and the growing influence of AI. So what happens if we do not adapt? Ignoring changing technology led to the demise of companies such as Nokia and Blackberry as Nokia failed to focus on software enhancements and Blackberry refused to change its platform. Abercrombie & Fitch ignored social trends and alienated customers with their "cool people" campaign. Concord failed due to costs, sonic booms, and lack of interior design for passenger comfort. Blockbuster dominated the VHS (Video Home System) market with film and video technology but ignored technology changes and social preferences, failing to join Netflix and transition to DVD online services.

Adapting our plans and companies to change is the key to resilience and a brighter future. In the Circles of Hope board and team meetings, participants practiced adaptability by asking what they liked and what they should change, or what they should start, stop, and continue doing. They gained insight into small things making a big difference in how our nonprofit provided services such as changing the time of meetings or scheduling outside events (Table 8.1).

Table 8.1 Meeting evaluation

Start	Stop	Continue
Board meetings from 5:00 to 6:00 p.m.	Missing meetings.	Focusing on improvements
Include pastors of nearby churches	Resisting change to service offerings	Growing a rainy day fund

I do much writing in my local library. The librarians keep in touch with their surroundings and continually adapt to changing circumstances. After the turmoil of the pandemic, their practices returned to prepandemic norms—no more distancing, no masks, and back to regular schedules. This summer, COVID-19 rose in our community and librarians shifted again. Some now wear masks and maintain plastic shields between them and visitors. They continuously adapt to technology changes as well. Technical specialists train them on equipment upgrades and social media changes, and are weaving AI into their sessions. Each of these organizations has strategies for growth but remains adaptable to clients' changing needs as they execute their plans. Failing to adapt is not an option to them.

How a Business Adapted

The Pressley Group adapted to COVID-19 by creating a new day and new way of leading and managing a business. Everyone in the agency participated in a retreat and designed a plan for adapting to constant change and uncertainty. They created a customer newsletter, daily and weekly communication, improved phone system, and lead generation tools. The first month after the retreat Jeremy's agents improved from 50 to 80 insurance sales. The following month two agents were out sick with COVID-19 and insurance sales improved from 80 to 83 units. Employees were working together to solve problems and create a more efficient operation. Over the next six months the Pressley Group began producing over 100 sales per month and hired two more agents. To continually adapt, Jeremy and Stephanie conducted daily Zoom meetings (15 minutes) with everyone in three counties. The Monday meeting was an hour long during which each agent reported their sales from the previous week and time was used for recognition and solving shared problems. Six months later, Jeremy's agency was producing over 100 units per month, while competitors were struggling to stay afloat. The agency's goal had been to increase production by 25 percent but it achieved 100 percent improvement.

Much has been told about the achievements of John Chambers. When he took the helm at Cisco in 1995, the company was primarily known for its routers and switches, with annual revenue of US$12 billion.

By the time Chambers stepped down two decades later, Cisco had become the backbone of the Internet, boasting revenues of nearly US$47 billion.

The message of this remarkable man to me is how to anticipate and prepare for disasters and unpredictability. From the beginning of Cisco's rise, Chambers would go through the work areas, soliciting ideas for making the business better. It has been told he would push a grocery cart with goodies, and when someone offered a good idea, he would give them a prize and encourage them to make their idea a reality. He was known for using a collaborative approach with his management team when dealing with crises, including the dot-com recession of 2000 to 2001. This approach enabled Cisco to make informed decisions rapidly and adjust resources to economic downturns. It was also key to Chambers' success at positioning the organization for future growth.

Whether leading a company of 70,000 employees worth billions or an agency of 10 employees worth six or seven figures the same ideas apply. Focusing on the needs of customers and collaboration with company human resources and management teams leads to faster response times for adapting to current disruptions, anticipating disruptions, and pouncing on opportunities to grow.

Five Questions

1. Companies fail to adapt because of:
   A. Communication with customers
   B. Not collaborating with workforce
   C. Management practices
   D. All of the above
2. How Jeremy adapted to COVID-19?
   A. Developed plans with employees
   B. Changed his way of managing
   C. All of the above
   D. None of the above
3. Adaptability includes:
   A. Doing things differently
   B. Organizing people
   C. Doing the same things the same way
   D. Having a stiff drink after work

4. Adaptability does not include:
   A. Internet searches
   B. Reliance on AI
   C. Monitoring trends in technology
   D. Monitoring social trends
5. John Chambers:
   A. Planned for disruption
   B. Elicited ideas from his workforce
   C. Elicited ideas from his management
   D. Elicited ideas from his customers

Answers, Strategy

Chapter 5	1 = B+C; 2 = A; 3 = C; 4 = B; 5 = A+C
Chapter 6	1 = B; 2 = D; 3 = A; 4 = B; 5 = A
Chapter 7	1 = A+B; 2 = C; 3 = B+D; 4 = B; 5 = B
Chapter 8	1 = B+C; 2 = C; 3 = A+B; 4 = B; 5 = A+B+C+D

PART 3

Practices

Now we understand why we should make changes in our companies to counter four recurring disruptions using a business model for doing so. Let's explore how others have strengthened their operations, financials, employees, and customers to achieve resiliency in their markets.

CHAPTER 9

Operations and Climate Disasters

Stories and statistics tell us it is time for a reset if we are to be fully prepared for more disruption from climate change. Learning from others and building efficiencies into our companies lead to greater resilience during the tempests we encounter.

Preparing for Disruption

We respond best to climate disasters by planning for future ones and creating highly efficient operations. The better we organize the people in our companies and communities for seamless production, the greater our ability becomes to rapidly react to the wildfires, floods, and hurricanes challenging our future well-being. We can mitigate the extent to which climate disasters impact our neighborhoods. We reduce damage when we reforest deforested areas with trees to break the intensity of soil erosion; when we use porous substances to absorb rainfall instead of concrete or asphalt in parking areas. Calvin Maye, a farmer in Sylva, North Carolina, learned from his county agricultural agent to let grass grow longer on hillsides to slow the water flow, to dig trenches and to place logs horizontally on the slopes to redirect water from pouring directly down banks, to reinforce stream banks, and to encourage trees and foliage along creeks to strengthen the banks and protect fish. In all these ways, we lessen the damage caused by climate disasters. Imagine the community that comes together to make and execute plans for dealing with climate challenges they encounter. We make things better when we anticipate events, and we make things worse when we pretend disruption will not happen again.

A neighbor, Nate Yoder, a successful executive with a business in Florida. Here are his thoughts:

There is not a 'one shoe fits all' when it comes to companies preparing for climate disasters. There are different approaches to take into consideration based on the type of climate disaster you are preparing for (i.e., hurricanes, tornadoes, blizzards, droughts, flooding, wildfires, etc.). On whether or not the company is private or public. On the company's geographic location (i.e., local, state, regional, national, or international). On whether it has one or many locations. On the number of personnel and on the type of industry.

Using Florida as an example, residents and businesses must prepare for hurricanes. Hurricanes are annual events that typically occur between June 1 and November 30. Living in Florida, it is not a matter of if but where. If you have a single location and are close to the coast or are located in a flood zone, you need to reinforce your building envelope with hurricane-resistant windows and doors and with metal roofing, and strap down your roof trusses. And you must develop a contingency plan should you need to evacuate, lose power or communications, or your building is destroyed. Where and how will you continue to operate? You also need to have a game plan for your workforce because, in manufacturing in particular, if your workforce is adversely impacted or experiences damaged or destroyed housing, the priority is survival and damage repair, not going to work (this happened to some of our workforce two years ago). If your building is destroyed, what is your backup plan? Where would you continue to operate from? How would you communicate with your staff to ensure that they are all okay? Do you have a muster point so that after the storm, and if communications are lost, there is a designated location for everyone to meet? After a climate disaster, the safety of your employees and their families or tending to their immediate situation (e.g., injuries, damage to personal property, evacuation) is the most important thing.

In other parts of the country, if you live in California, you must prepare for earthquakes, fires, and floods. If you live in the Midwest, you must prepare for tornadoes, floods, and blizzards. If you live in the Northeast, you must prepare for blizzards. If you live in the Gulf Coast region, you must prepare for hurricanes and rising sea levels. No matter where you are located, identifying the different scenarios and threats to your business and developing a game plan—and then doing a dry run to prepare with your team before any crisis occurs—are crucial.

Every company will have a different use for renewable energy based on their industry, market, and geographical location. Wind farms, hydroelectric, solar, and nuclear power are energy options, but at what cost or disadvantage compared to conventional fossil fuel sources? If you are a publicly traded company (which is brutal these days) depending on your industry and market, renewable energy may be worth exploring. However, the reality is that it may also present a competitive disadvantage if producing products that compete against ones coming from India, China, or Russia, or against other companies that do not care about climate issues. Your shareholders and Wall Street will demand that you provide a return on investment, and introducing a new technology or alternative fuel that may be more costly but environmentally beneficial could lead to losses, which may result in hostile takeover attempts by rogue investors or to the ousting of a CEO who is trying to do good. That said, every company needs to try to develop environmentally friendly alternatives and options that result in being good environmental stewards, yet remain lean and competitive in the process. This can be accomplished, but a publicly traded company can never forget that its shareholders invested in good faith to make a financial return. Private companies have more flexibility in this area and should continuously address environmental issues, whether in production, operations, or within the community.

Another neighbor, Peter Holmberg, lives part of the year on Saint Thomas in the U.S. Virgin Islands where he races boats in the Caribbean. He shared thoughts on growing up in the islands.

The climate risk we face is the growing intensity of hurricanes. This affects all aspects of life here, from strengthening our homes to survive the higher winds to coping with the aftermath. We observed where structures failed, and changed our home designs and building materials to counter this. Once the renewable energy technology improved, we started switching over. In the past we all had generators, but then when storms cut off our supply lines, fuel became the problem. Many of us have now installed solar panels and batteries to our homes and now we can be energy self-sufficient.

All these steps have made us a more efficient society, consuming fewer fossil fuels, using renewable energy, and becoming more self-sufficient. A great side effect is that disasters and setbacks help bring a community closer together. We are forced to cooperate, help rebuild a neighbor's house; it reminds us of how it used to be, and of how good it is.

After personally going through three major hurricanes, and in 1995 losing my office, home, and race boat, I felt it firsthand. And, interestingly enough, I can honestly say that our islands are a better place after going through hurricanes, forcing us to pause, reconsider how we go forward (rebuild), and bringing us closer together as a society. As someone who lost a lot, even I appreciated the hardship (once it was all over!). We also now stop and better prepare before storms come; not ignoring the warnings, but taking them seriously. This prevents greater damage.

Business Practices

Nate Yoder observed that remaining lean and competitive is critical to sustainability in the face of growing challenges. In fact, companies and communities who practice certain tools and talents become more adaptable. Tools include organizing people into mastermind groups for decision making and problem solving, and managing projects with scorecards and action plans for project implementation. Talents include the ability to facilitate, communicate, and celebrate improvements

Companies respond to the increasing frequency and intensity of climate disasters with strategies focused on renewable energy, reducing pollution, improving risk response, and developing more efficient operations. Efficiency occurs when managers organize and engage workers in running effective operations. Mastermind groups, pioneered by Dr. Edward Deming and Toyota when creating the "Toyota Way," are the foundation of efficient operations.

Mastermind Groups

Even in today's world, too many companies remain in the past, managing individual accountability and using outdated 20th-century models. They experience difficulty reacting to change and retaining staff in today's labor shortage. Successful leaders who organize people and develop management teams to collaborate and communicate make a critical difference in their company's ability to operate effectively. A group structure supported by enabling systems including performance management tools, recruitment and retention programs, and pay and promotion policies coupled with progressive management, magically increase quality, cut costs, and respond to disruptions including climate disasters.

These concepts are used in both companies and communities. In communities, leaders gather to help one another solve problems and achieve their goals. The governors of New York, New Jersey, and Connecticut worked together during the COVID-19 pandemic to share resources and improve regional communication serves as an example of a successful community initiative. In companies, people are organized into mastermind groups in every department to become more efficient and respond rapidly to changing circumstances.

Mastermind groups share a common vision and goals for running their part of the operation. Every group's vision and goals are aligned with company goals. The groups meet regularly and collaborate as a team to enhance the products, services, and processes within their responsibilities and to hold each other accountable to their commitments. The ideal size of these groups varies from three to 12 members. Typically, groups meet weekly to brainstorm solutions to issues, encourage and support one another, and set challenging goals. Goal setting, problem solving, action planning, and celebration of success become the foundation for these groups to succeed within companies that excel.

Mastermind groups take one of three forms: functional groups consist of members who perform similar tasks; cross-functional groups perform different tasks that are dependent on one another; and multifunctional groups have members who can perform multiple tasks that are required of the group. For example, functional Group A makes widgets and functional Group B makes tokens. These groups become cross-functional when members of groups A and B work together. Multifunctional groups have members from both groups A and B who can perform both tasks and make widgets and tokens. For smooth transitions into a group structure, the team interviews candidates and makes hiring recommendations. They become responsible for onboarding and training new hires,

When working for a software development company, I replaced the human resource (HR) deputy who resigned to start his own business. Our staff was challenged to react to needs within a company growing rapidly from 600 to 1,000 engineers and led by a controlling CEO. Our HR department included recruiting, training, benefits, salary administration, and market research. Our director created silos in our department by meeting with us separately each week.

My first change was to break down silos and create greater communication by meeting with our staff together each week. I recognized that how we made decisions in our meetings would matter. I had a choice of "Direct" decision making in which I would make all decisions and give directions to staff. Or I could use "Involve" decision making in which I would solicit the ideas of staff before I made a decision. Another choice would be to "Engage" the staff by being one voice and vote when making decisions. I could "Empower" my staff to make the decision and let them handle implementation of their ideas. In our first meeting I involved my staff. They offered ideas that were developed into a mission statement. I made the final decision on what the statement included. The following week, we developed goals with each HR team member that aligned with our mission statement. I asked them to set goals for their responsibilities. As each offered ideas, we discussed the pros and cons and I made final approval of each person's goals. The next week I changed my decision option and engaged everyone. I asked them to decide on a reward when we met our monthly goals. We discussed options and agreed to go to lunch together. I would hire a part-time person to cover the office. I was careful to be part of the decision instead of being the final voice. We all agreed on the idea together with a show of hands. Part of the agreement was if we failed to meet our goals, we did not go to lunch together. By engaging and involving my staff we formed into a functional work group in which members began learning each other's responsibilities.

Once we began consistently achieving our goals, I involved the team in a discussion about what they would like to learn. They expressed interest in knowing more about each other's job duties. I invited them to pair with someone else and cross-train each other. Over the next six months, staff members began sharing ideas and filling in when their partner was absent. They became a multifunctional work group in which each person performs other jobs in the department. They supported one another and I was proud of them. At the end of my second year, I informed everyone that I planned to take a two-week vacation. I empowered my team. I asked them to run our department as though I were there and keep my desk clear. I gave members signing authority for their areas of responsibility and left on vacation. When I returned, my desk was clear; I was shocked! They had become a multifunctional work group.

The team successfully progressed through the four stages of group development: forming, storming, norming, and performing. My group formed when we started meeting together. After several weeks we began storming when we did not meet our goals and go to lunch. There was blaming of the person who failed to meet their goal and of me for refusing to take the others to lunch. After several more weeks we were back to the norming stage when meeting and sharing with one another. By the final stage of performing, we were meeting our goals consistently and cross-training each other. The group had become highly efficient. We were able to rapidly make informed decisions and perform at a high level even when one or two people were absent. My greatest lesson learned from this experience was how important it is to be able to adapt my decision making to the growth and challenges of my staff. That is a lesson I continue to share with others.

Every group must go through each of these four stages to achieve higher levels of performance. Should a new member join the group, retraining must occur. Should a member leave the group, responsibilities change. In both situations, the four stages of development begin again. So how did this efficiency help in times of change? My role changed to being an ambassador for our department and I spent time with the company's management team. I learned of changes affecting us before they occurred. For example, I learned that our company was being purchased. I immediately notified our group. In our weekly meeting we formed plans to meet with our counterparts in the acquiring company and build relationships. During the acquisition I was told our team had been the only department able to make the necessary changes quickly.

Within the year, I was recruited by the Miller Howard Consulting Group. I was intrigued by their ability to turn companies around and save jobs.

Internal Supply Chain

After my training, I was assigned to serve Printpack in Atlanta, Georgia. The company provided film to Frito Lay for packaging food products and was dedicated to achieving greater quality and operational efficiency.

A design team made up of union members and management restructured the facility into work groups. The maintenance team performed maintenance on the equipment, the setup team prepped the machines to run film, the production team processed the film through the machines, and the packaging team packed and shipped to customers. Each team became part of a supply chain within the plant. The maintenance team interviewed the setup and operations teams to learn their needs. The setup team interviewed the operations team to create better ways to assist them. The operations team interviewed the packaging team to learn their needs. Each of these teams developed scorecards to measure their success in satisfying their internal customers. A representative of each team interviewed the company's external customers to better understand their requirements.

This new operational structure created major improvements in production and customer service. As the production team made decisions on equipment placement, improved production methods, and waste reduction, magic happened. Supplies and materials were moved closer to the production equipment, and each team worked more closely together. Both management and operation teams began making decisions together. This new culture was an involved process in which the team leader led discussions with the group before making a decision. This approach soon morphed into a collaborative model in which the manager and group discussed and agreed on the final decision together. This model worked well as teams began rearranging equipment and supplies to become more efficient.

Cycle time on each product line was reduced by more than 60 percent, while errors and waste were cut in half. Clients were better served and happier with faster delivery of higher-quality film. Employees were happier and more productive. This production facility increased efficiencies, cut costs, and reacted rapidly to customer change requests.

That structure and process provide companies and communities the ability to respond to climate disasters and other disruptions, just as Printpack responded to clients rapidly and efficiently.

Breaking Down Silos

Increasing operation efficiency means changing the manner in which people are organized. One of McDonald's goals was to increase market dominance by building 30 restaurants in a year. Two departments were responsible for new restaurant development: Real estate project managers purchased land on which construction project managers designed and built restaurants. Construction engineers blamed real estate managers for poor land choices. Real estate managers blamed engineers for being demanding and inflexible. In their best year these two groups constructed seven restaurants. Their story offers a classic example of the magic that creates efficiency when silos are eradicated and people pull together.

The real estate manager was being transferred to Hong Kong. As a first step to breaking down silos, I suggested the construction manager, Bob, lead both real estate and construction departments. There was general agreement with the reminder to build 30 restaurants with existing staff. For this goal, Dave Natysin promised that everyone on the project and their families would earn a vacation to Hawaii if they achieved their daunting goal. Bob and I took both departments off-site for a two-day retreat. In that retreat we agreed that all decisions must be agreed on by all members. The meeting began by creating a shared vision. The participants analyzed their work processes and were surprised to learn their processes were very similar. After extended discussion, they reorganized engineers and project managers into two multifunctional mastermind groups consisting of real estate, construction, and administrative personnel.

They developed a plan and measures to guide their progress. These measures included weekly updates on building costs and number of restaurants built. They agreed that one group would work on the east side of the Potomac and the other team on the west side. They chose leaders for each team and agreed on weekly and monthly meeting times and locations and how they would celebrate when they met monthly goals. Bob became the coordinator and resource provider of two teams of highly capable people.

These two mastermind groups began meeting weekly to review scorecards and plan the upcoming week. In their meetings, members updated one another, made adjustments, and planned their upcoming week. One of many innovations was to include building contractors in these meetings. Over time, project managers and contractors got to know each other well enough for contractors to work on-site without company supervision.

The teams began delegating decisions and tasks to their contractors. Previously, the project managers used a directive model in which they were on-site, authorizing tasks and making decisions. These duties became the sole responsibility of the contractors, who could order materials and coordinate tasks as needed. Building construction picked up speed.

Another innovation involved project managers partnering with suppliers to process maps and improving delivery times and accuracy. That reduced construction time even further. At the end of each month, the two teams met to review and chart total building completions and costs before going out to lunch together. By year's end they had not built seven but 32 restaurants! They outperformed every region in the country. Most importantly, that record was set with the same number of people in the team as in prior years. The team increased capacity and market share across its Washington, DC market. These awesome people and their families enjoyed their week in Hawaii.

Innovation

My work with McDonald's was complete, and my next assignment was Air Canada's maintenance operation in Montreal, Canada. During my time there we designed and implemented mastermind teams with goals and measures across the total maintenance group of 3000 hardy union brothers and sisters. During that time productivity and efficiencies increased and costs were reduced. Additionally, grievances completely stopped. After nearly two years I was asked to serve the Winnipeg maintenance station. Bill, the operations manager, had heard of the positive changes in Montreal and requested help in Winnipeg, where temperatures dropped as low as −8°C. Bill was a big man with thick black hair, a matching black beard, and deep voice. At six two and 250 pounds, he appeared formidable and could have been intimidating had it not been for his quick wit, easy laugh, and sincere wish to make things better for the union colleagues at the base. He had worked his way from union member to shift supervisor, foreman, and eventually station manager.

Bill's first wish was for forepersons and union stewards to communicate and cooperate. So my challenge was training both union stewards and company management together. They practiced listening skills in which forepersons listened to union stewards and vice versa. Bill and the union president participated in these meetings. In his weekly union–management meeting, Bill led problem-solving sessions. He asked his team to share any rumors circulating around the base. The rumors were sorted through to determine true from false. After these meetings a union–management team visited union meetings to share the truth. Management and union maintenance workers were all organized into mastermind groups and trained to collaborate and solve problems in their meetings. The structure enabled communication to occur rapidly and accurately across the base.

Bill did something remarkable. He mentioned that he was going to design a new laboratory for the station. I asked what he thought of putting the technicians in charge of designing their lab. Several weeks later, Bill invited me to join him at the grand opening. The laboratory sparkled with new tables and equipment arranged in circles in each half of the room. Bill explained that he had delegated everything to his technicians.

They designed their space to facilitate a smooth workflow and to bring special skills to special projects. Each side of the room was organized to accommodate specific research activities coupled with brainstorming and decision making. Bill admitted he would never have conceived of such an arrangement.

Several months later, Bill announced that the base had won maintenance contracts with two airlines. These airlines audited the Winnipeg base and awarded contracts based on the efficiency they observed.

As Air Canada transformed from government-owned to publicly traded, the Winnipeg station grew its market share through greater efficiency and higher-quality services using mastermind groups. The groups were facilitated by managers who were trained to guide discussions and to keep brainstorming moving and discussions on track. The groups had codes of conduct to guide them in their meetings. Additionally, agendas were created with input from these groups. Finally, action plans were completed at the end of each meeting and published to group members on the same day.

Accountability was positive and improvements were celebrated. When members were not meeting their goals, others asked how they might help. Group meetings were early in the week to review the past week's actions and plan for the week ahead. Information was passed through the company every week, enhancing companywide communication, its ability to respond rapidly to changing requirements, reduce or eliminate waste and errors, and improve maintenance productivity.

How Air Canada and Others Solve Problems

The purpose of mastermind meetings is to resolve issues, reduce waste and costs, and increase efficiency. This is a time-tested model for solving problems and comprises the following steps.

- Pinpoint the problem. We succeed when we define the problem in measurable terms. For example, a site manager walking through the machine shop spots a pile of sawdust on the floor. The number of times sawdust is found on the floor may be the measure.

- Analyze causes. The site manager asks a machine operator five "whys" to understand the problem.

  SITE MANAGER: "Why is sawdust on the floor?"

  OPERATOR: "The motor we were working on was leaking oil."

  SITE MANAGER: "Why was the motor leaking oil?"

  OPERATOR: "Several motors from this supplier have leaked."

  SITE MANAGER: "Why are motors from this supplier leaking?"

  OPERATOR: "Faulty drain plugs."

  SITE MANAGER: "Why haven't I been told about this?"

  OPERATOR: "I have no idea."

  SITE MANAGER: "Why are we using this supplier?"

  OPERATOR: "Purchasing was offered a lower price than our last supplier."

  If the site manager had used only one question, the sawdust on the floor may have been swept up but would have continued to appear.

- Identify solutions. Once the causes are known, solutions can be developed. For example:

  SITE MANAGER: "Who should I talk to in purchasing?"

  OPERATOR: "Joe."

  SITE MANAGER: "What did you do with the motor?"

  OPERATOR: "It's on the shipping dock to be returned to the supplier."

  Here, both the site manager and machine operator participate in developing the solution.

- Implement solutions. The following day the site manager walked through the shipping area and could not find the motor. He asked an operator, who explained that they had decided to keep it and use its parts when repairing other motors. The site manager informed the crew that purchasing would use their old supplier on future orders. Both the manager and machine operator implemented reasonable solutions.

- Evaluate. Monitor measures to determine whether solutions work. No more sawdust on the plant floor. Problem solved.

For companies to adapt and compete in today's ever-changing climate, their operations change from relying on individual performance to bringing employees together and using their ideas.

Leaders like Dave Natysn at McDonald's, with a new vision for their business, encourage collaboration. Each restaurant or profit center alone would not be able to accomplish challenging goals, but by working together in a new operational structure they succeeded. The benefit of engaging every part of the organization, involving all staff in information sharing and decision making, led to better and more creative decisions. Efficiency, productivity, and the ability to rapidly react to disruption were enhanced. The McDonald's Washington, DC region improved from last of the U.S. regions to first as their market share soared during a slow economy.

In summary, as we encounter increasing environmental catastrophes from floods, extreme storms and heat, wildfires, and tornadoes we find ourselves in a better position to react and respond when it is our turn to encounter disasters. As our Florida businessperson, Nate Yoder, observed, those who are lean and efficient are best prepared to survive and thrive during times of distress. Just as the Pressley Group faced difficulties during the pandemic, the ability to collaborate with others and solve problems together makes a difference in companies and communities when disasters are overwhelming. Other companies representing financial services, manufacturing, and retail have also experienced excitement as income grows and people adapt within ever-changing business ecosystems.

As Governor Roy Cooper observed in the Report on Hurricane Helene Recovery, implementing national building codes in North Carolina could save $11 for every $1 investment. Seeking ways to mitigate damage could save $6 for every $1 invested. Becoming highly efficient and preparing now for future disasters is critical for sustaining our communities and companies. Daniel Swan, the climate scientist focused on the dynamics and impacts of extreme events, has observed that we have the tools and ability to mitigate and reverse climate change but there is no will to do so politically. The solution is to elect representatives who will take steps toward mitigating climate disruption and reversing global warming.

Five Questions

1. Responding to climate disasters does not include:
   A. Planning for more disasters
   B. Finding fault
   C. Organizing people
   D. Finding ways to be efficient
2. Air Canada increased its efficiency by:
   A. Training management to be more assertive with union members
   B. Training union stewards and management to communicate together
   C. Keeping rumors quiet
   D. Organizing union and management into work groups
3. Nate Yoder prepares for climate disasters by:
   A. Having contractors on standby
   B. Having a communication plan for sending employees home
   C. Having a backup facility
   D. Tending to immediate needs of employees
4. Building efficient companies does not include:
   A. Collaboration
   B. Eliminating meetings to cut costs
   C. Solving problems
   D. Training employees to make decisions
5. Peter Holmberg's community does not:
   A. Update plans together
   B. Change home design and building codes
   C. Use generators for power outages
   D. Install solar panels with batteries

CHAPTER 10

Financials and Political Actions

Anxiety abounds when political administrations change in Washington, DC, and new policies influence our companies and communities. We have learned how political actions lead to financial hardships and company failures. Strengthening the financial component of our companies leads to healthy enterprises during the uncertainty of government action and inaction. No matter whether it is a one-person coffee shop or a company employing thousands, the same principles apply. Businesses underperform or go under due to financial mismanagement. A coffee shop owner was unable to describe his monthly profit margins, failed to keep track of income, and did not pay state taxes. The state shut down the business. Deregulation of energy markets in the 1990s allowed companies to place bets on future energy prices. Enron saw an opportunity and changed its accounting practices to count future projections as revenue. It collapsed from financial mismanagement. Its auditor, Arthur Andersen, went bankrupt when audited by the SEC. A nonprofit was led by a director who monitored income and paid bills on time. When she retired, the organization was on a firm foundation. The new director focused on services and public relations, did not track account balances, and ignored overdue bills. The organization collapsed when an audit uncovered unpaid bills and inadequate funds in its account.

Most of us are not guilty of mismanagement but may be challenged to make the most of what we have. Leaders own the responsibility to achieve greater operational income by either increasing their top line or reducing the bottom line, preferably both. Several of the tools and talents described earlier (e.g., mastermind groups, performance measures, and problem solving) are used to manage and improve financial performance

using the hands and minds of the workforce, rather than mass terminations for a quick fix. So let's learn from those who have experienced
greater success.

Business Integrity

The recessions of 2001 and 2008 would not have occurred if certain
business leaders had balanced their principles with their drive for
greater wealth. Instead, they lost all sense of ethics as they took advantage of less regulation to increase their financial positions with Wall
Street. Ethics is thought of as conforming to principles of right versus
wrong. It has been seen as how one person treats another, how your
behavior affects others and how corporate behavior affects communities. Someone observed that morality is defined as how we treat people
we know and ethics defined as how we treat people we do not know. To
establish cultures of ethics and integrity companies develop controls
rewarding ethical behavior and punishing cheating behaviors within
their organizations. It was news when a peanut butter company's CEO
was criminally convicted of wrongdoing. The conviction of a CEO was
so rare that it was seen as newsworthy. To avoid jail time and thrive
in uncertainty nine leadership behaviors create cultures of principles
and wealth.

1. Prominently display company principles and financial performance.
   Keeping everyone in the know about the business leads to a culture
   of ethics and financial success.
2. Keep staff current on organizational plans and activities. For your
   staff to make better decisions they need to be aware of company
   actions and decisions.
3. Provide needed information to staff. Learn from employees what
   they require from you to perform their duties and let them know
   what you need from them. Update them on progress toward goal
   attainment and business accomplishments.
4. Be honest and direct with staff. Share good and bad news and provide time for discussion. Giving your honest assessment builds trust
   and ethical outcomes.

5. Do not shoot the messenger. A software development director fired his project manager when she described problems completing the project on time. Such behavior creates a culture of fear and truth avoidance.

6. Encourage free flow of information. An open climate for communication and building trust is created when associates are encouraged to openly share information and discuss projects.

7. Encourage staff to challenge the status quo. A culture of innovation is established when a leader thanks those who challenge their thoughts. Listening and rephrasing encourages sharing of ideas when creating a workplace of integrity and ethical behavior.

8. Respond rapidly to staff concerns. Employees learn to trust their leaders when they request assistance. Let them know how you can help and when you will deliver.

9. When upset, speak calmly. Associates are easily intimidated by loud voices and use of profanity (Box 10.1).

Box 10.1 Integrity summary

1. Display principles and financial performance
2. Keep staff current
3. Provide information to staff
4. Be honest and direct
5. Don't shoot the messenger
6. Encourage information flow
7. Challenge status quo
8. Rapidly respond to concerns
9. Speak calmly

Business Practices

From Competition to Cooperation

McDonald's Washington, DC region, the largest of 40 U.S. regions, was seeking ways to grow in the slow economy of the early 1990s. The company's practice was to meet weekly with profit center managers. Each manager reviewed their sales and food and labor costs and were questioned when they failed to meet goals. The meetings were tense; managers dreaded Monday mornings. The region was ranked number 40, last place in the United States, and the pressure was intense to perform better, much better. No matter how hard managers tried. No matter how much pressure was applied. The region remained in last place.

I attended these meetings. One Monday morning I was asked what I would do. "Instead of looking at the past and identifying fault, why not look forward and solve problems getting in your way?" I asked. Heads began nodding around the room. Dave Natysin, nodded in agreement. The following week Dave started the meeting by asking managers to share successes and disappointments from the prior week. They were asked to share problems preventing them from succeeding in their markets. They relaxed a bit and risked discussing problems affecting their profit centers. With a little coaxing they began offering ideas to help each other. At the conclusion of the meeting, Dave asked them to focus on one problem in their market and return the following week prepared to offer ideas for improvement. At the next meeting, smiles on many faces, the managers filed into the conference room. The room was filled, not with tension but with excitement. Dave asked for reports, after which he congratulated each manager on their initiatives and reviewed the region's numbers. Regional sales were flat, but they accomplished a slight reduction in costs. That was just the beginning!

Dave experienced improvements in sales and cost numbers as he encouraged his managers to collaborate with each other, their restaurant managers and crew members to solve problems. They rolled out a new team structure throughout their profit centers and managers were trained to listen and facilitate their groups. They implemented scorecards and goals from each profit center to every restaurant shift team. Each team was trained to solve problems and excite their customers. Instead of comparing their performance against each other, they began to evaluate and improve their performance by learning from each other. Rather than competing against themselves, they began a fierce competition with their largest competitor, Roy Rogers. Over the next two years, the Washington, DC region rose from worst to first as these managers increased sales while reducing costs and staff turnover. Staff turnover reduced as crew members and restaurant supervisors were included in problem solving and received recognition as sales and costs improved. Dave and his management team began helping other regions and, in turn, his own region improved. Trust and cohesion grew as they solved problems together. Dave created a resilient region during an uncertain economy.

Strategy and Leadership

How did leadership and strategy within a low-margin paper manufacturing company increase income and cut costs? I was consulting with a fiberglass manufacturer who made space suits for NASA. My assignment was to build in quality throughout their plants. In the manufacturer's North Georgia plant, the teams decided to replace their supplier, Star Paper Tube, because of quality problems with their tubes. As a result of losing this major client, Star Paper Tube contacted our firm and I was chosen to consult with its corporate office in Rock Hill, South Carolina.

We began by developing a strategy for improving the company's operations and market position. Two rigorous days of reflection and change became the turning point for how these executives chose to manage their company and employees. They posted their vision and mission in the corporate office lobby for everyone to see. Several weeks later I was told the company had closed two deals after prospective clients toured their offices and commented on Star Paper Tube's vision. Revenue began to increase.

The next step was to design a model production facility for manufacturing a higher-quality product at a lower cost. During the design process, one of the team members, a senior machine operator, offered the opinion that one of the ideas would not work in existing plants. The operations vice president was in the room and overheard him. After the session, he pulled me aside and excitedly said, "Joe sounded just like a manager in there." His opinion of his workers changed after listening to their ideas and comments. Later, mastermind groups were implemented across the production facilities. Each group was given responsibility for improving quality and reducing production costs. The supervisors were trained to collaborate and problem solve with their groups. Several months later I was contacted with great news. The company was on track to save

$750,000 in its first year of change! This low-margin company had increased its margins with higher sales revenues and reduced production costs. It had achieved resilience in a highly competitive market.

Increasing Income

Tools and talents used to improve financials include scorecards, engagement, problem solving, and positive reinforcement. Roy, a neighbor of ours, invited me to tour his veterinary clinic. The first thing I noticed was two graphs on the wall next to the reception desk. One graph was labeled "Sales" and the other "Expenses." The grooming area had two graphs titled "Customer Count" and "Customer Satisfaction." "It looks like the lines are going in the wrong direction," I observed. "We know," Roy said. "The young man working here moved in with the young woman we recently hired. They have been arguing over the last few weeks. Several staff members have talked with them, and we believe things have been worked out." In the operating room two graphs were also posted, tracking "Customer Count" and "Customer Satisfaction."

I examined the two graphs behind the front desk. Each graph reported weekly data for a year and tracked seven years of comparative data. The sales graph illustrated that every year, revenue was higher than the year before. The expenses graph told a different story. The lines increased steadily for the first several years before flattening out and remaining relatively stable over the last four years. "Weren't you concerned your staff would know how much money you make?" I asked. "No, they thought I was rich," he chuckled. Roy experienced seven years of steady income growth while containing his costs. He had beaten the odds of many entrepreneurs.

Roy described a class he had taken during his first year in business. He learned the importance of keeping everyone focused with graphs and using positive reinforcement. His reinforcement, 10 cents on every dollar the clinic earned over the same period the previous year, became a monthly bonus. Employees chose how to spend their bonus. "That is why my staff talked to the couple about their work performance," he explained. We really began moving forward when we initiated annual planning sessions. We meet outside of work each year to update our plans and make changes," he shared. I could see the pride written all over his face as he smiled. So the combination of scorecards coupled with positive reinforcement (10 cents out of every dollar earned over the same time the previous year), decision making, and problem solving by staff and total inclusion in annual plans and weekly business huddles resulted in everyone becoming part of the business and seven years of steady income growth.

Roy learned that to increase sales, reduce waste and costs, or reduce absences and tardiness, verbal and visual feedback are necessary. Another small-business owner had recently charted his business performance for the past two years. These graphs reported weekly data for sales, customer counts, and expenses. In doing this, the business owner realized for the first time that customer counts were lower than for the same time the previous year. Further, while sales receipts indicated higher sales, inventory cost increases masked actual income, which was trending downward.

Over several years, a Chick fil-A operator's income eroded as competing restaurants moved into the same intersection. He decided it was time to make changes. He closed his restaurant and met with his crew and family one morning. They received training on managing data, collaborating, and problem solving. Approximately 40 crew members and managers brainstormed ways to increase revenues. The owner chose to be one vote in their decisions, and all staff agreed on a plan to increase the average check amount on customer orders. They developed methods to upsell, reorganized into shift teams, developed a scorecard to track sales, and crew leaders agreed to call out hourly sales totals to their teams. The following month, the average check amount increased by $1.00 per order and continued to improve over subsequent months. Revenue soared. The owner's daughter presented their initiative in a class project at her community college and won first place.

Reducing Costs

The plant manager of Printpack's Atlanta plant was experiencing excessive supply costs. His costs had mushroomed over three years to more than $250,000 annually. He decided to use the talents of his mastermind groups to find a solution. He met with mechanic and machine operator teams together and delegated complete management of plant supplies to them. Each group was provided with storage containers and locks and asked to develop supply budgets for the upcoming year. Their budget totaled $100,000. Throughout the year, these work groups met and reviewed their numbers, monitored usage, and ordered supplies as needed. The year-end budget reconciliation reported a total plant supply expense of $50,000. These mechanics and machine operators reduced costs by over $200,000 in their first year. Their leader trusted them, and they repaid that trust by managing supplies and cutting costs for the company.

Shell USA, Inc. began involving frontline workers in decision making, including when making changes to their offshore platforms. Typically, Shell's management team created the annual budget. This time, using mastermind groups, managers asked their operations teams to develop the budget. Operators researched their expenses and resources and proposed a budget that was lower than their current year's budget. At the end of the following year, costs were $250 million less than the prior year. The process of using mastermind groups for involving and engaging workers was used in Shell's Canadian operation and was credited for saving their production facility from shutdown.

Air Canada's Montreal maintenance group performed various maintenance inspections on their aircraft, The most complex of these inspections was referred to as the H check. The H check involved taking apart the whole aircraft, inspecting, enhancing, and replacing parts before reassembling the aircraft. The completion time for H checks was typically 135 days. The standard was 75 days. It had never been achieved. But that was to change! One cold winter morning the H check maintenance foreman, a tall lanky fellow, began using the skills he had learned in class to facilitate his mastermind maintenance team. He called all three crews together and, using a flip chart, facilitated brainstorming ways to improve their work. He encouraged his crews to disregard the existing process for H checks. Crew members talked and the foreman asked questions, writing notes on the flip chart. They spent nearly two hours brainstorming until they reached agreement on a better way to perform H checks. Their next H check was completed in a record 72 days!

How did this miracle happen? First, the foreman changed and used the tools and skills of brainstorming and problem solving. Before a final decision, each person, including the foreman, voted and they all had to be in agreement. The three union crews recognized that each crew would wait for the previous one to complete its work before proceeding with its duties. For example, the crew inspecting and repairing seating waited for the electrical team to finish before reinstalling passenger seats. During brainstorming they realized that some projects could be completed in tandem. Seats could be installed in one section of the aircraft while electrical systems were installed in another. They coordinated and communicated during their assignments so effectively that they set a maintenance record, cut labor costs, improved efficiency and quality, and increased revenue by returning aircraft into operation sooner. They knew how much better they were performing because the foreman posted graphs in the work area for crews to monitor and celebrate. Similar projects began springing up in other parts of the facility, increasing efficiency and reducing costs across Air Canada's Montreal base.

Hidden Cost of Turnover

Employee turnover is a hidden cost. Turnover is the rate at which employees leave an organization and are replaced. It is measured as voluntary, involuntary, and total turnover. When people quit, there is lost production time, burnout, and lower quality of work as others pick up the slack. The cost of training another person and managers redirecting their focus to hiring activities also contribute to less efficiency. Cost of a termination ranges from half an annual salary for nonexempt employees to twice the annual salary of highly skilled exempt employees.

The annual staff turnover rate in the United States ranges from 24 percent to more than 50 percent. On average, companies lose 18 percent of their workforce each year, of which 12 percent is voluntary and 6 percent is involuntary. A turnover rate exceeding 10 percent is considered excessive for optimum operational performance. Of those who quit, 31 percent leave within the first six months of starting a job. In 2022, the overall cost of voluntary employee turnover in the United States amounted to more than $1 trillion.

Reducing terminations offers a major cost reduction opportunity and happier people. McDonald's DC region achieved a 10 percent reduction in overall costs. Part of that cost saving was achieved by reducing crew turnover by 66 percent and management turnover by 50 percent.

Step 1: Measure Turnover

Solving labor turnover costs requires an accurate turnover count. As a consultant once observed, "You can't change what you can't measure." Here is how to measure staff turnover.

Calculate the annualized turnover to evaluate the effects of changes and establish a baseline for accountability. An example, turnover calculation from January through April. On January 1, the company employed 30 people. During the four months through April the company employed as many as 35 people. Eight employees quit.

1. Calculate the average number of employees for the four-month period:
   Add the number of employees at the end of each month: 30 + 33 + 32 + 35 = 130
       Divide 130 by 4 months = 32.5 average head count per month
2. Calculate the annualize turnover rate:
   Divide 8 (number of terminated employees) by 32.5 (average number of employees) = 0.246
       Multiply 0.246 × 100 = 24.6 percent (annualized turnover rate)

Step 2: Create a Culture of Inclusion and Engagement

McDonald's managers were taught to listen to staff, to include them when planning and developing goals, to collaborate with them when making decisions and solving problems, and to inspire them with rewards and recognition for goal attainment and continuous improvement. Such practices include involving employees in decisions about recruitment and retention initiatives and decisions regarding hybrid work practices for work and family harmony.

Step 3: Labor Stabilization

In weekly meetings managers and supervisors report on employees who have recently quit and on anyone they anticipate leaving, as well as on their plans to retain them. Persons who were not expected to leave but did are discussed to problem solve how managers can better forecast leavers and develop action plans to retain and develop them instead. For additional accountability weekly or monthly reports on annualized staff turnover in each department provide a greater sense of urgency for reducing staff turnover.

Step 4: Onboarding Sessions

The purpose of 12 weekly one-hour sessions is to enable new hires to adapt to their new culture and to network with other people. They learn about policies and procedures and the duties of each part of the company, they receive recognition for work accomplishments, and they enjoy engaging with one another and participating in fun activities together. Companies who use this onboarding model with labor-stabilization meetings significantly reduce staff turnover rates and labor costs.

My lesson learned is that, whether preparing for a workout or helping companies improve financial performance, we achieve success when counting, recording, and setting targets for what we wish to achieve. I recovered from a long illness. I am slowly regaining my strength by counting my daily reps I take for bodybuilding and measuring my distance and time when I run to rebuild endurance. My wife and Harvey the dog know how much I improve my numbers every day. The more open we are with ourselves, our families, or employees regarding financial status, the more opportunities we have to achieve more income. And when the parts of our organizations work together rather than compete, they sustain and grow regardless of how federal and state policy impact finance and operations (Box 10.2).

Box 10.2 Turnover reduction steps

1. Measure turnover
2. Inclusion and engagement
3. Labor stabilization
4. Onboarding

Five Questions

1. Business integrity includes:
   A. Maintaining confidentiality of financial information
   B. Providing information on a "Need to Know" basis
   C. Displaying financial information and principles
   D. All of the above

2. McDonald's largest region improved costs and sales by:
   A. Ensuring greater accountability on profit center management
   B. Placing the weakest managers placed on progressive discipline
   C. Encouraging managers to help each other
   D. All of the above

3. A low-margin paper tube company increased sales and profits with:
   A. A competitive strategy
   B. Progressive discipline for operators who created excessive waste
   C. Employee work teams
   D. All of the above

4. A Chick-fil-A restaurant increased income by:
   A. Reducing number of associates on each shift
   B. Reducing number of waffle fries in a box
   C. Closing the restaurant for planning
   D. Upselling customers

5. Shell USA reduced costs by:
   A. Directing operators to cut costs
   B. Reducing the number of operators on night shift
   C. Using operators to develop annual budget
   D. All of the above

CHAPTER 11

Employees and Social Complexity

Studies reveal that social threats to companies and communities are effectively managed by how companies attract, retain, and grow workforces that bring in customers and keep them coming back. Resilience is derived from our workforce. We can revive a new spirit that leads to company growth or discourage our employees by the systems we put in place and the management practices we use. This chapter offers human resource practices to address the social problems many companies encounter with both employees and customers.

Recruit

An opportunity to gain a competitive edge for the best and brightest employees exists when recruiting candidates. With a shrinking labor supply and increasingly diverse population, a successful endeavor utilizes a hiring team of employees from the work area in need of staff. This team includes people of various ages and races. Their purpose is to interview candidates, inform them of the work expectations and duties, and make recommendations to the hiring manager. Candidates learn the good, the bad, and the ugly of work responsibilities and, if hired, how the company will onboard them. For example, the business owner of a pet supply business trained staff to conduct interviews. They conducted the first round of interviews before the owner interviewed their recommended candidate and made the hiring decision.

Hiring teams should follow EEOC guidelines to avoid discriminatory practices (https://www.eeoc.gov/us). Candidates should not be asked about potential disabilities, medications they take, or workers' compensation claims. Discussions are permitted with applicants who have disclosed a disability or who may require a change to the working environment or to the way a job is usually done if a reasonable accommodation is required to perform the job. Applicants may be asked to voluntarily report a disability for affirmative action purposes. Different rules apply after a job offer is made and after the employee starts work.

Title II of the Genetic Information Nondiscrimination Act of 2008 Report prohibits use of genetic information in making employment decisions and in any aspect of employment including hiring, firing, pay, job assignments, promotions, layoffs, training, benefits, or any other term or condition of employment. Applicants cannot be asked about family medical history, genetic tests, or genetic counseling. For example, you cannot ask an applicant about a close relative's heart condition, mental health conditions in the family, or genetic tests to determine cancer risk.

These rules apply to any communications with or about the applicant, including application forms, interviews, and reference checks. They apply whether seeking information from the applicant or someone else, such as the applicant's doctor, former employers, friends, or family. Avoid asking applicants about personal characteristics that are protected by law, such as race or color, religion, sex, national origin, and age. Avoid topics around being biracial, religion, language(s) spoken at home, age, and an applicant's pregnancy or plans to start a family.

Following these EEOC guidelines may prevent litigation and creates a sense of professionalism and fairness with applicants. The pet supply owner reviewed these guidelines with his staff before asking them to interview candidates. He told me that the person recommended by his staff had not been his first choice; however, he accepted their recommendation. His staff implemented an onboarding process, resulting in this new employee performing better than other new hires in the past. He grinned as he explained how things worked out.

Jeremy Pressley, of the Pressley Group, whom we met earlier, also agreed to accept his staff's recommendation when hiring. He expressed concern about one of the candidates based on her track record. After a slow start, this new employee became agent of the month and Jeremy was very happy to watch his agency's sales increase. These and larger businesses that involve their employees when hiring attract needed staff from limited pools of talent in their communities.

New-hire onboarding is critical to an effective hiring strategy. Starting a new job creates uncertainty and excitement on the part of a new hire. They are in a foreign culture with written and unwritten rules. Estimates of the time it takes for people to adapt vary from one week to one year. Effective onboarding consists of 12 weekly one-hour sessions. Topics include policy reviews, management expectations, and project goals, along with fun activities such as *Wheel of Fortune* or *Jeopardy!* Supervisors attend these meetings and offer positive recognition of workers in their organization. There are two benefits of this approach: First, onboarded members get to know others in their group and develop a support network. Second, new employees become familiar with the rules of the road sooner and tend to remain rather than not returning to work.

Retain

When contemplating employee retention there are certain policies and practices to avoid:

- Demands for long working hours with unpaid overtime. This leads to dissatisfaction, low morale, and increased workplace tension.
- Inconsistent and untrained managers. They are more likely to give inconsistent feedback, discipline, recognition, and work assignments, leading to resentment throughout the workforce.
- Little opportunity for growth or personal development creates feelings of being undervalued and underutilized. Workers in such situations seek opportunities in competing companies for personal growth.
- Low pay and benefits lead to employee discontent. The lack of pay raises or cost of living adjustments creates low morale and dissatisfaction. Inadequate health insurance and retirement plans communicate that the organization is not financially sound and creates employee unrest.
- Pay and promotion practices favoring certain cultures or genders. This leads to resentment and conflict and results in staff turnover and class action lawsuits.

An informal survey revealed the reasons employees remain with a company. They seek cultures that help workers achieve personal and professional goals, provide competitive pay and benefits, and encourage workplace harmony. A Pew Research report, "How Americans View Their Jobs" (March 30, 2023), by Juliana Menasce Horowitz and Kim Parker found that "Most are highly satisfied with their relationship with their co-workers and manager, but relatively few feel the same about their pay, opportunities for promotion." The survey of American workers reported satisfaction levels of 62 percent for relationships with manager, 51 percent job assignments, 49 percent feedback, 49 percent benefits, 44 percent training opportunities, 34 percent compensation, and 33 percent opportunities for promotion. Clearly there are a lot of dissatisfied employees if only two scores are above 50 percent. These are all management issues, contributing to national turnover rates ranging from 30 to 50 percent. Greater staff retention means less hiring and training, less disruption serving customers, reduced error rates, and lower costs.

Managers can create a happy and productive workforce by listening to staff and including them when planning and developing goals, by collaborating with them when making decisions and resolving conflicts, and by inspiring teams with rewards and recognition for continuous improvement and goal achievement. Another opportunity for inclusion involves employee participation when developing recruitment and retention initiatives and creating hybrid work practices. McDonald's used a four-page orientation package listing 12 ways employees could be terminated. The human resource manager decided to be positive and created a one-page policy statement describing five ways to grow within McDonald's. The management-related skills used by McDonald's and other successful enterprises for employee retention include the following.

Communication

Employee retention begins with communication, a process involving a sender, a message, and a receiver. The receiver confirms receipt of the message, creating a feedback loop with the sender. Rephrasing and questions are used to clarify understanding, learn more, and connect with the sender. The most effective questions are open including who, what, why, where, when, and how.

I was training managers for the Eastern Band of Cherokee Indians and a construction supervisor became a star pupil. After learning to listen, he started conducting Monday morning meetings with his crew. He asked, "What do you need to do your jobs better?" They responded, "New boots!" Many had boots that leaked and made working uncomfortable. He got them new boots. At their next meeting he asked, "What do you need to have a good week?" They responded, "We don't have the tools we need in our trucks." He suggested they take the first hour of the shift to survey their trucks, order any missing tools, and get organized. The following Monday the supervisor reported in class that his crew leader told him, "We know you have class today, but don't worry. We have everything taken care of." Not only did they take care of everything, but crew production improved!" he said with a grin. Today's managers excel to the extent they engage their people in how work is performed, as this construction superstar learned.

Bob Doret, change leader for Air Canada's maintenance operation, shared a story one snowy afternoon. When walking through the terminal to his office on a Friday morning, he met an old friend. "Hello, John. You don't seem to be feeling well today. What's wrong?" Bob asked. John told him about problems at home and at work and continued talking until they reached an intersection, each going a separate way. As they parted, Bob said to John, "It sounds like things are pretty rough for you. I hope they get better soon. And tell me if I can help." John came to Bob's office the following Monday morning to say, "Bob, you are the only person who has shown any interest in me, and I thank you." Such is the power of listening. Bob used an open question followed by a long silence. He listened, offered an empathic statement and to help, and became a closer friend. Regardless of the nature of your company, you have a much better chance of retaining your people by listening first and showing empathy (Box 11.1).

Box 11.1 Communication process

1. Open Questions
2. Silence
3. Rephrase
4. Empathy

Collaboration

Companies who seek ways to retain workers and improve productivity do so by including them when making decisions and solving problems. My son left a software company after six months of being micromanaged. His project manager met with him every morning, asked him to describe his actions from the prior day, and gave him his next assignment with instructions. I left a family-owned consulting practice because a partner insisted that I provide daily reports, assigned people to work with me without notifying me, and failed to inform the assigned person or me about the purpose of the visit.

Collaboration involves making choices. The software company manager used a "Direct" approach in which she did the telling and my son did the doing. She could have "Involved" her team in decision making by meeting with them together and requesting their ideas on assignments and completion goals. Alternatively, she could have "Engaged" them by offering assignments and permitting team members to discuss and chose assignments. Or she could have "Empowered" her group by giving them full authority to assign duties and set completion goals among themselves. My son may have remained if his project manager had met with him weekly, encouraged him to share his experiences, recognized tasks he performed well, and offered assignment choices.

Similarly, the consulting partner could have met with her consultants together weekly, discussed current activities, and solicited ideas on upcoming projects and persons to work with. Both companies would have lower staff turnover and better outcomes if project teams met weekly to collaborate, discuss lessons learned, receive recognition for good work, and share ideas on upcoming assignments. Basic tools for communicating and collaborating center around the following (Box 11.2).

Box 11.2 Deliberation options

1. Direct
2. Involve
3. Engage
4. Empower

Meeting Frequency

Problems crop up consistently. The frequency with which employees work in groups and meet to resolve pressing issues matters. The purpose of mastermind group meetings is to share information, recognize progress on projects, solve problems, and continually improve. The longer the time between meetings, the more issues to be resolved. Meetings are most effective when conducted consistently at the same location, on the same day, and at the same time. The length of meetings depends on their frequency. For example, weekly meetings last one hour, biweekly meetings last two hours, and monthly meetings require as much as four hours. The longer a group waits to meet, the more time it requires to resolve more issues.

The McDonald's real estate and construction teams met weekly for an hour. Most of their time focused on solving problems and planning work for the upcoming week. Their monthly meeting, in which both groups met together, lasted closer to three hours as they reflected on the past month and developed actions for the next month. Their plans included sharing resources, such as loaning an engineer or project manager to the other team.

Code of Conduct

A set of guidelines is helpful for keeping meetings running smoothly. A list of behaviors created to guide group behavior in meetings is referred to as a code of conduct. It is developed during the early formation of a group and has been proven to create trust and to begin bonding. Some examples of behaviors include:

1. What is said here stays here
2. Start and end on time
3. No interrupting
4. No heat-seeking missiles

If a code is violated, a team member calls out the code of conduct number for all to hear. Typically, the group will get back on track. For example, should a team member interrupt another person who is speaking, someone would call out, "Number 3." Members check the code of conduct and the interruptions stop.

Growing People

Tools for growing employees include performance reviews and compensation. You may recall earlier research that pay practices vary based on employee race, gender, and age. Such practices create tension, resentment, and lots of vacancies. Using salary ladders based on living wage data. (Visit https://livingwage.mit.edu/ to find current living wage data for every U.S. county.) This data can be used as a guidepost to eradicate racial and gender disparities in order to retain and grow needed talent. Compensation plans use a midpoint for determining salary ranges. Using the living wage as the midpoint in salary ranges can make a company more competitive when recruiting and growing its workforce.

Feedback systems can be used to develop staff by providing feedback on past performance to guide future performance, reward performance, and remedy discriminatory practices. Feedback is most effective when it immediately follows a behavior. Annual reviews are delayed feedback and have minor impact on personal behavior. Over the past two decades a variety of performance management options have become available.

Continuous Feedback

The consulting firm Deloitte reviews individual and group performance after every project or quarter. Based on their reviews, people are assigned to upcoming projects with clear goals to help them improve and excel. The benefit of continuous feedback is that employees are consistently updated on their work and can swiftly adapt and grow. Feedback and rewards are provided in such a way as to impact individual performance and grow people (www.deloitte.com).

Team Evaluation

Today's workforce is more diverse and talented requiring more collaboration and involvement, achieved by team structures and functions. For example, McDonald's appraisal system rewarded individual production achievements. However, as the company began working in teams, this goal discouraged members from orienting new staff. Because members were paid based on individual production, they lost production time and money if they shifted attention to helping new team members. The feedback and pay systems were modified to reward team members for orienting new recruits on working together to achieve goals.

People are evaluated based on the achievement of company and team goals and results. Team objectives measure and track milestones such as the scheduled number of monthly and annual production units for the team. Google uses this method as part of its growth strategy. The benefit of developing team goals that are aligned with company strategy is that team members focus on working together to achieve common goals. Team members grow as they share and learn from one another and the business grows as well. Team evaluations occur as frequently as weekly or monthly based on how data is reported and scorecards are updated.

360-Degree Team Feedback

The 360-degree team performance appraisal is based on team member performance input from team members, support staff, customers, and possibly others who can offer insights. For team leaders and managers, team members provide input for their appraisals. Companies find 360-degree team feedback helpful for developing managers and team members. This approach also offers a broader array of feedback to correct pay and discriminatory practices. For example, Netflix is doing away with annual individual performance evaluations in favor of 360-degree team reviews that provide broader perspectives of team member capabilities.

Individual Evaluation

Managers create work objectives with employees that are aligned with department and company goals. Goal setting is outcome-based using a business performance matrix or strategy. For example, a business goal of increasing market share may lead to an individual goal of enhancing the company's website. Individual evaluation of achieving these goals occurs annually or semiannually. The length of time between performance and feedback offers minimum impact on workforce growth due to the lag time between performance and feedback. This approach remains popular for businesses managing individual rather than group performance.

Stacked Ranking

An outlier system, developed by Jack Welch, CEO at General Electric, was created in the late 20th century to resolve issues with conventional performance management systems. Employees are compared against each other rather than against achievement of objectives. For example, 20 workers are ranked 1 through 20 based on how their performance is seen compared with their coworkers. They are grouped along a bell curve identifying the best, those in the middle, and worst performers. Those falling in the worst performers portion are terminated or put on performance improvement plans.

When employees are rated against one another, they compete to look good and to make their coworkers look bad. The process creates conflict among team members, lowers production, leads to bad publicity, and results in excessive staff turnover. The practice has been used by as much as 20 percent of corporate America, including Oracle, Amazon, General Electric, Google, Microsoft, and Goldman Sachs. Microsoft and Goldman Sachs discarded the program and so has General Electric. It has been said that forced ranking is the best method to turn around a struggling company. In fact, nothing could be further from the truth. There is no evidence supporting the claim. Ask Jack Welch.

Corrective Feedback

Continuous feedback can help people develop and grow when used by managers in daily contact with their employees. When an employee is underperforming, corrective feedback is helpful. Tim Richardson, area director at COUNTRY Financial Market 6, used the corrective feedback model to correct an agent who complained about changes to his

---

Box 11.3 Corrective feedback model

1. When you
2. Consequence
3. Your feelings
4. Their solution

---

compensation package. Here is how Tim used corrective feedback to handle the situation:

When you: "Joe, when you complain to others about changes we are making,"

The consequence: "it leads to discontent and sales production suffers."

How it makes me feel: "I get frustrated as our numbers drop."`

The solution: "What do you suggest we do to fix the situation?"

Joe apologized and offered to help other agents improve their sales and to recruit a new agent. Tim Richardson grew one of his best agents and improved sales production as well (Box 11.3).

Motivate High Performance

Positive reinforcement is defined as a consequence that maintains or strengthens behavior, and is a critical tool for developing people and companies. One of my clients was the 3M company. I was consulting with their manufacturing plant in Guin, Alabama where the management learned the power of positive reinforcement. Each shift in the plant set up scorecards measuring quality and production. Machine operators were asked to set goals for their shift performance and decide how to celebrate improvements. The agreement was to cater lunch for improvements and a long lunch with extra time when goals were achieved. Additionally, supervisors and managers learned to complement operators with "attaboys" for taking initiative and improving how work was performed. We had no idea how much better performance had become until two engineers from Minnesota visited the facility to conduct an audit. The audit was requested because this plant exceeded all production standards. No facility exceeded production standards before Guin did so. The plant manager credited the effort for avoiding an impending labor strike. My next assignment was 3M plants in Freehold, New Jersey. Five actions motivate and grow others regardless of age or culture:

1. Catch someone doing something good every day.
2. Use four times more positive than corrective feedback (4:1 ratio).
3. Be specific and use data when celebrating success.
4. Be sincere.
5. Offer praise for even a 0.1 percent improvement (Box 11.4).

Positive feedback works when people improve their performance. So when employees are improving, even just a smidgen, be sure to offer positive feedback. Verbal recognition to motivate an employee looks something like this.

When you: "Jane, your production has improved over last month."
The consequence: "Others in your group have noticed."
How it makes me feel: "It's great seeing your progress!"
Offer praise: "Your extra effort is appreciated."

Create Win/Win

Many of us do not like conflict. Workplaces are evolving as more generations are employed along with increased cultural participation by Asian, African American, Hispanic, and Native American workers. Women are playing a greater role in the world of work. These differences combined

---

Box 11.4 Steps to motivate

1. Catch someone doing good
2. Four times more positive feedback
3. Use data to celebrate success
4. Be sincere
5. Recognize a 0.1% improvement

with various preferences for performing work create conflict. Unless issues are readily resolved employees become distracted and grumpy. A process is available to help management convert conflict to cooperation. The good news is that achieving cooperation takes only three steps along with lots of patience.

1. Identify the Needs of Each Person

People in conflict want to be heard. Be sure only one person talks at a time. The tendency is to tell what they want, not what they need. For example, a conflict exists between two employees: Heather and Mohammed. The manager asks Heather to describe her needs and Mohammed to remain quiet and listen. Heather wants Mohammed to leave the department. Mohammed wants Heather to leave. Manager asks Heather more and learns she feels insulted by some of his remarks. Mohammed confides that he does not like comments Heather says about him behind his back. The needs are now clear. Each person is offended by comments of the other.

2. Brainstorm Solutions to the Needs

The manager takes a deep breath and leads a brainstorming exercise to find solutions to each need. Heather is encouraged to find solutions to Mohammed's needs and Mohammed is guided to seek solutions to Heather's needs. The manager uses a white board or flip chart to record their ideas in their own words. Heather and Mohammed are encouraged to remain respectful of the other. When they completed offering solutions, the manager asked them to select solutions meeting both needs. Mohammed was surprised to learn he had offended Heather and agreed to refrain from using certain phrases. Heather agreed to talk about Mohammed only to his face.

3. Make an Action Plan

The concluding step is completing an action plan. Remember what are the steps that are agreed upon, who will commit to enacting each step, and when they agree to complete their actions.

Heather and Mohammed agreed to the following—What: Discontinue using certain words and speak to one another face to face. Who: Mohammed and Heather. When: They agreed to meet with manager in two weeks to evaluate progress.

Our Home Owners Association needed our road improved. Heavy rain damaged our gravel road. Ditches needed cleaning and widening. Gravel was needed on most of the road and grading the gravel was required. We have an annual budget that must be managed as well. After gravel and grading we used nearly half the budget.

A road crew member contacted a contractor to clean and open our ditches. The cost would have cut the rest of our budget in half. I objected to the cost and asked for alternatives that would preserve our budget. After some push back from neighbors, several alternatives were offered including using a local crew to clean the ditches and use the contractor at the end of the year based on our remaining budget. When everyone agreed on this solution we proceeded. When the ditches were clear I asked everyone if they were satisfied. They were and we still have money remaining for the remainder of the year. No matter whether in companies or communities these talents prove useful in today's world of uncertainty (Box 11.5).

Upskilling and Reskilling

How we develop a spirit and develop our employees impacts our ability to adapt not only to social disruption but also to disruptive technology. It matters how companies grow their workforce and management teams to successfully use new and evolving technologies and soft skills. As we have discussed, today's labor supply is shrinking, more diverse, and aging. New skill requirements prompted by social media and AI are leading to

---

Box 11.5 From conflict to win/win

1. Identify the needs of each person
2. Brainstorm solutions
3. Devise an action plan

companies upskilling and reskilling their workforce. To compete for staff, grow employees, and secure new business, companies are encouraging employees to list their duties and what they see as next steps in their careers. A full inventory of existing and new skills can identify gaps and development opportunities. This information is used to determine new jobs and capabilities linked to changing technology and new product introductions.

Employees are aware of the need to adapt and have a vested interest in developing new skills. For that reason, training programs should be designed with input from employees. Successful programs will design skill development initiatives based on employees' learning objectives. To best use the time of both trainers and learners, it is advisable to provide on-the-job training. This way, learners experience how their new talents apply directly to their jobs.

Adult Learning

Developing tools and talents for managers and employees is accomplished using adult learning concepts. Developed in 1968 by Malcolm Knowles, the theory refers to the concept of adult learning and how it differs from childhood education. According to Knowles, five key assumptions exist for developing and delivering adult education: self-concept, adult learner experience, readiness to learn, orientation of learning, and motivation to learn.

1. Self-Concept. People in the workforce are independent and may be trained in a self-directed approach. Adults exercise more control and responsibility over their personal lives and education. I conducted an Entrepreneur's Academy, sponsored by the Haywood Chamber of Commerce. Students were asked to name their learning goals at the beginning of the first workshop. Afterward, they develop a code of conduct for how they choose to participate and interact in four workshops. At the end of each workshop, the class is asked to evaluate their learning experience and offer ideas for improving at the next workshop. They have control.

2. Adult Experience. Adults draw from their knowledge and experiences. Adult education centers around experiential exercises and discussion of lessons learned. Group participation is encouraged using their life experiences. For example, a college professor organized her students into groups of three to share their experiences about accessing community resources. They performed research in their groups and chose which resources to investigate. When training entrepreneurs, I ask participants to fill out a chart representing their four business components. Students add ideas for each quadrant and discuss with each other how to improve their companies.

3. Readiness to Learn. Adults learn for a reason. As employees assume new responsibilities, their learning requirements focus on new tools and talents. They need to see how the learning relates directly to their problems and tasks. For example, a regional director of the Alzheimer's Association was new at her job. She was ready to learn and asked if I could improve communication within the agency. I nodded and asked to meet with her and her staff to design a learning program. I listened to their issues and missteps and offered ideas to address conflicts, people underperforming, and miscommunication. Everyone participated in developing an agenda and appeared eager to learn.

4. Orientation to Learn. Memorizing facts and information does not work for adults. They want learning that helps them solve problems and work more effectively. Learning should be applicable to their lives and implemented immediately. They need logic to absorb information. They want to be involved in planning their training. They want to control what, when, and how they learn. A client wanted greater efficiency in her company. We designed problem-solving workshops in which participants developed listening talents and cause-analysis tools. During the workshop, participants practiced diagnosing their efficiency problems. After gaining proficiency in class, these adult learners applied those skills at work and became more efficient.

5. Motivation to Learn. As children, we are taught based on the learning goals of our parents and teachers. Adults learn for their own reasons, such as how to use new technology in their jobs or develop

a new hobby in pursuit of new activities and skills. They become motivated to learn as they perceive how certain skills and knowledge can directly aid them achieve their goals of mastering new technology or a new hobby. Western Carolina University's College of Business combines a didactic teaching approach with experiential learning. Highly motivated students are organized into small groups with assignments to interview businesses, develop presentations of lessons learned, and present findings to their class. They learn business practices experientially and theoretically (Box 11.6).

When employed by a software development company, I was tasked with training software engineers to train their customers. We recruited five engineers. In our planning meetings we discussed how adults need to see, hear, and touch to learn new talents and how they prefer to have a say in what they learn and how they learn. Over several weeks we created a two-day seminar on how to install and run an investment software system. We recruited several development engineers to be a practice class.

In our class, these engineers were asked to interview the person on their left and identify their learning goals. After two minutes, they switched to learn about their partner's goals. Students then reported their learning goals to the class. We posted their goals on the whiteboard and made their goals our teaching goals. Then, instructors gave a 30-minute overview of the four-module system and how to use the technical manual. The class was then organized into two learning groups. The groups were asked to review their technical manuals and decide how they would install and run Module A. They were given 30 minutes to prepare for class reports. Both groups presented workable action plans for their assignment.

Box 11.6 Designing training for adults

1. Self-concept
2. Adult experience
3. Ready to learn
4. Orientation to learn
5. Motivation to learn

On the first day, we completed group discussions and learning about the system functions and deliverables. On the second day we asked for feedback before beginning the day's activities and made adjustments. Our key learning was to be clearer with our instructions. Class assignment was to install a module on our system. After making their plans, each team presented their ideas before plunging into installation. At the conclusion of the practice workshop, we asked our engineers to point out anything we should stop, start, and continue doing for public classes. After several adjustments we were ready to go live. In each class we requested feedback to continue improving our workshops. I remember the first time an instructor called to tell me that clients were requesting on-site training. That was a big deal!

In summary, if we are to achieve resilience in today's turbulence, it becomes incumbent on us all to consider how we recruit, retain, and grow our asset that goes home at night and may not return the next day. Doing the same things the same way with our personnel will not make it in a society composed of diversity, disruption, and changing values.

Five Questions

1. Recruiting practices should consider:
   A. Today's limited labor supply
   B. People do not want to work
   C. People's values are changing
   D. All of the above
2. From employees' perspective, what do they expect from managers?
   A. Give desirable work assignments
   B. Provide satisfactory compensation and benefits
   C. Offer promotional opportunities
   D. None of the above
3. Employee retention requires:
   A. Management accountability
   B. Listening to different points of view
   C. Collaboration with workers
   D. All of the above

4. Growing personnel includes:
   A. Annual performance reviews
   B. Corrective feedback
   C. Catch people doing good
   D. All of the above
5. Employee training should:
   A. Use adult experiences in class design
   B. Ask employees what they want to learn
   C. Develop data memorization ability
   D. All of the above

CHAPTER 12

Customers and Technology Change

Achieving resilience is how we deal with our reason for existing in business, our customers. Rapidly changing technology has changed the calculus on how we communicate and relate with customers. It may be helpful to define who consumers, customers, and clients are. Consumers are found by companies through capturing our data, marketing information to us, and feeding us information that can be either true, misleading, or both. To these enterprises, we are consumers, faceless and price points to be manipulated. Amazon, Facebook, and Google are examples of companies that interact with us as consumers. Customers are people in places such McDonald's and Chick-fil-A with whom employees connect face-to-face and establish relationships that help the businesses grow. Clients are people taking part in business-to-business transactions, such as the software development company that I worked for. Our clients were people in the insurance industry. Our software development engineers, market specialists, and management team developed relationships with our clients as we served their needs. Each of these individuals had the responsibility for growing the company's business.

If you have consumers, viewed as blips on a computer screen, you can stop reading. However, if you have responsibility for increasing customer counts, grab a cup of coffee and join me.

Building a Business

My business education began at the University of North Carolina, Chapel Hill. It was not in class but during summers when I sold *Webster's New World Dictionary* door-to-door for the Southwestern

Company in Nashville, Tennessee. My first summer I sold to families with school age children in Decatur, Georgia. The second summer, I recruited a crew of students and sold in Omaha, Nebraska, where I earned the President's Award for selling 104 books in a week. I earned enough money to pay for another year at UNC and to buy my first car, a blue Ford Fairlane 500. Over four summers I learned valuable lessons that help me today in business, even as I write this book—such as to never give up; to set and achieve goals; to continue to improve as a father, husband, and person; and to work hard at whatever comes my way. My lessons learned about building a business include the following.

Product Knowledge

When selling dictionaries, I learned eight definitions for the letter "A" and my dictionary had more words than other dictionaries. I could tell stories about the stories in the back of the book. In my current work as a business consultant, I learn about a prospect's needs and practice my questions before meeting with them about how we might solve problems together for having a resilient company and a brighter future. For example, I recently asked a prospect about her goals and what obstacles she experienced getting in her way. We were able to make a plan for working together after I considered her situation, conducted research and offered a proposal for helping her attain her goals.

Sales Conversion Ratio

Know your conversion rate and remember that every no takes you closer to yes. It is possible to remain motivated when we know how any no it takes to get a yes. My ratio was one sale for every four sales calls. I rarely called on four homes and got a sale, but the number of calls in a day averaged one sale for every four calls I made. I remember working long days, sunup to sundown, knocking on doors and selling only one or two books. But I knew that if I tried just as hard the next day, I would make my sales ratio. I always did.

Credibility

I was a total stranger meeting the person answering the door. Using names of friends and neighbors gave me instant credibility. "Good morning, Mrs. Jones, my name is Ron Robinson. I was just talking with Mrs. Johnson up the street and she suggested I talk to you. May I come in for just a minute?" Rarely was I turned down. When I was not invited inside, I presented the world's greatest dictionary through the screen door and would sometimes surprise myself with the number of sales made that way.

Product Features

Features are the information describing those parts of the service or product that help the customer. For example, my dictionary not only had more words but had a picture section depicting classic stories about legendary people like Daniel Boon. I learned to use questions leading to a yes before describing each feature. "So, Mrs. Jones, wouldn't it help Johnny to have a resource for his book reports? Let me show you these short stories that are helping other students his age." Asking closed questions during a review of features leads to yes when asking for the business.

Product Benefits

Selling the sizzle brings in more business. I did this by describing how the book helped little Sally develop her vocabulary. "So this updated word content was what helped Sally increase her vocabulary and earn better grades in her Language Arts class. The stories in the back provide ideas for book reports they will write this year." Or I might tell a customer how it helped Bobby and Jenny get better grades. "Mrs. Collins bought two dictionaries to help Bobby and Jenny improve their grades this year."

Ask for Agreement

The greatest failure we make when building our businesses is not asking for the business. Always ask for the business as you finish describing the benefits of your products or services. Check for agreement then ask for the sale. "Mrs. Jones, wouldn't you agree this dictionary can help Johnny in school? Would you like to get your dictionary today or wait for delivery in August?" Today I might ask, "Would you rather begin next week or the start of next month?"

Welcome Objections

There were always objections. Be prepared for them. Rarely would a prospect buy on the first attempt to close. They usually had at least one of the following objections. They still do!

Objection: "I don't have money."

Response: "I understand. Mrs. Smith said the same thing. She realized the book could really help her children, so she ordered a dictionary to be delivered in August and put a $3 deposit on it. How much of a deposit would you like to make?"

Objection: "We have a dictionary."

Response: "I am sure it is helpful. As Mrs. Thompson observed, her dictionary was five years old and new words are added to dictionaries every year. She made space next to her old dictionary and bought a book yesterday. Would you prefer to get your dictionary today or in August?"

Objection: "My husband is not home."

Response: "It is great that you make decisions together. Mrs. Thompson felt the same way but she knows her husband wants the best for their children so she got her dictionary yesterday. I imagine your husband wants the best for your children and would be happy to have an up-to-date dictionary for his use as well. Wouldn't you agree? So, I have dictionaries in my car. How many would you like to get today?"

Consultative Selling

The sales process used in my college years does not work in today's world. A more collaborative approach provides greater power when communicating with multiple generations, cultures, ages, and needs. The next story describes an approach for today's businesses that combines the best from past and present sales models.

During the pandemic Cary Heidesch was laid off by Men's Wearhouse. He chose to start his own business using his data analysis talents. We discussed goals for his first year in business, which were to acquire four clients and generate $80,000 in sales. Cary's homework was to develop goals for each part of his business (financials, operations, customers, and family) set weekly sales-call goals; and write weekly activities on his calendar. He posted the calendar in the kitchen to coordinate activities with his wife.

To secure four clients, we developed an elevator pitch. An introduction of two to three sentences explaining how clients benefit from a product or service is an elevator pitch. We developed a process for getting appointments while at chambers of commerce events and Rotary meetings. Cary would strike up a conversation with the people on either side of him at his table. He would say, "I help businesses and institutions use their data to increase income. The Seattle Seahawks increased attendance and sales, and St. John's University increased donations. Would you like to increase your revenue? Great, when can we get together?" Cary started getting appointments. As he gained entry to prospective clients, we practiced a consultative sales model including build rapport, establish goals, ask and advise, close for commitment, and have a record.

Build Rapport

Find something you and the prospect have in common. I was helping Cary during the COVID-19 pandemic. Using Zoom, I observed the awards on Cary's wall and learned that Cary was a North Carolina State graduate and won awards for his work using data analytics. He observed that I was a UNC graduate and live on a mountain. Cary began scanning the offices of his prospects for clues to their backgrounds and sources of pride. He found subjects that he and his prospect had in common and was able to build rapport and start relationships.

Establish Goals

Our next discussion involved setting goals for the meeting. It helped Cary to be clear with his prospects about expectations and provided a means for him to uncover hidden agendas on the part of a prospect. As an example, I arranged to meet with a prospect. After we toured the offices of her business, I asked what she would like to accomplish in our meeting. She wanted to describe her last board meeting and the goals they had given her for the upcoming year. That information provided the opening for me to learn about her needs for help.

Ask and Advise Prospects

I never begin with a long explanation of what I do. I use open questions to first learn about the prospect. Cary and I practiced using open questions to learn about the needs of others and rephrased to confirm that we understood. For example, Cary asked a prospect, "What has this year been like? What would you like to see be better at the end of next year?" I asked my prospect, "What challenges do you face achieving the goals set by your board?" She described difficulties recruiting staff and leading a rapidly growing organization.

Describe Features

You may remember this technique from dictionary days. Cary asked his prospect, "Would it help to learn client purchasing patterns? I will analyze your marketing data and organize customer preferences." With my prospect, I asked how she would describe the performance of each of her staff. I rephrased her concerns with several of her new hires and then described how leaders improve workplace performance using tools and talents for communication, collaboration, motivation, and innovation. I asked if she agreed these could help her. She said yes.

Advise by Describing Benefits

Selling the sizzle involves drawing a picture of how clients get better using your products and services. For example, Cary described how St. John's

University experienced a 70 percent increase in donations over three years and how the Seattle Seahawks increased season ticket sales by using data analytics. With my prospect, I described how a client used communication talents to increase production in his business and another used collaboration to reduce costs and how a client involved everyone in creating a strategy for a brighter future and increased sales from 29 percent to over 100 percent of goals.

Close for Agreement

Some things never change from the book selling days. We ask for business using closed questions. Assume they want your help. For example, when I asked my prospect if she agreed these skills could help her program, she shook her head in agreement. Cary asked a client if she agreed that data analysis could help her. She agreed. He asked when she would like to start, and she suggested a date in the middle of the following month. I asked my prospect, "When would you like to begin?" We started two weeks later.

Cary quickly caught on. We continued to practice asking for the sale by offering choices: "Should we begin this week or next?" "Would you rather pay by debit card or cash?" and so on. He began contacting three businesses a day and closed four sales as we concluded our work together

Have a Record

When Cary returned to his office, he sent a brief e-mail thanking his client and summarizing their agreement. When I coach clients, I always send them a summary of our work within 24 hours. In summary, practice the power of listening and rephrasing what you hear. Present services and discuss features that address your prospect's needs. Sell the sizzle! Describe the benefits they will receive, ask questions that elicit a yes response, and give them a choice of project start dates or purchasing options. Be prepared to respond to objections and remind prospects of the benefits they will receive. Always follow up with a message thanking prospects and clients for their time and summarizing points of agreement. These ideas increase sales production in any company and are ideal for owners and managers who juggle activities and grow their customer base (Box 12.1).

Box 12.1 Steps to consultative selling

1. Build rapport
2. Establish goals
3. Ask and advise
4. Close for agreement
5. Have a record

Delight Customers

After more than 45 years having my own businesses and working with businesses and nonprofits, I learned 10 principles for delighting customers.

1.   Ensuring Quality

Associates are aware of customer needs. I ask clients to evaluate my service on a scale of one to five stars. When a client rates me four stars, I ask how I can earn five. When I am rated a five star, I ask how I can become a six star. We best serve customers when we focus on efficiency, quality, and customer feedback. Air Canada maintenance group's mission was to improve service quality. As its managers analyzed workflow and simplified processes, they realized that greater efficiency on their part meant that their customers were more satisfied when they received services sooner and with higher quality.

Amazon started its own trucking fleet to create greater delivery efficiency and become more competitive. Toyota and Honda set standards for quality production and now dominate their markets. Both auto companies focus on doing it right by engaging their total workforce to provide quality checks and quality assurance. They use teams in which everyone is expected to use both their minds and hands at work. These mastermind groups meet regularly to assess and resolve work issues and to celebrate successes. First-line associates stop production as soon as they spot a problem. Once the cause is diagnosed and corrected, production begins again. Managers wear the same uniforms as associates to signify that everyone is working together in mind and spirit.

William Styles, an insurance broker, designed a survey for his customers. Once office staff began surveying customers, they found many to be dissatisfied. As William listened and showed understanding, customers revealed other needs. Over the next six months, William began growing his book of business with much happier customers. Customers were given his cell phone number and staff were always available.

2. Gaining Product Knowledge

Knowing your products will lead to satisfied customers and greater sales. I needed supplies for my dog and stopped by a pet supply store. When I asked the person behind the counter to show me dog chews, she put down her phone long enough to take me to a station stocked with dog toys, then returned to the counter and her phone. I wandered through the store and walked out. She did not look up. When employees know products well enough to take care of customers, businesses increase income.

My first job was selling medical supplies for American Hospital Supply in Western North Carolina. My focus was on basic health care needs such as sutures, syringes, and other disposable products. My district manager trained me to use equipment for diagnosing cancer and how to present disposable surgical gowns for greater patient safety. My sales increased and hospitals were happier with my services.

One day our Shark vacuum cleaner stopped working. I called headquarters and a real person answered the phone. They asked questions such as, "When did it stop? Where did you buy it? What is the number on the plug?" The service agent identified the purchase date, informed me the machine was still under warranty, and issued a replacement while we talked. He diagnosed the problem and put a replacement in the mail the same day.

3. Providing Rapid Response

Cycle time is defined as the elapsed time from a customer's request to receipt of the requested product or service. When employees are aware of their cycle times and are trained to meet customer needs within those cycle time standards, customers are happier.

Research by the National Retail Federation reports that dwell time in grocery stores is at a new low of 17 to 18 minutes. Whether shopping in store or online, customers are impatient and expect rapid service. Continental Airlines struggled to gain market share and improve stock value. A new CEO changed the game when he empowered frontline employees to satisfy customer complaints without management approval. Each service unit was given a budget to rapidly address customer issues, grow the business and merge with United Airlines.

An opportunity exists to improve customer service centers. The excessive time customers waste going through numerous automated instructions, waiting for someone to answer, attempting to understand accents, then being sent to another person, creates frustration and horror stories. Those who use real people to answer the phone delight customers with speedy service. Enable customer service agents to move quickly to other experts and managers for solutions. Train agents to address communication difficulties with customers at the beginning of discussions. When tempted to replace humans with AI for resolving customer issues, remember the warnings of Geoffery Hinton and Sam Altman about questionable outcome quality when relying solely on AI.

4. Communicating Effectively

Person-to-person communication is necessary to delight customers. Technology, outsourcing, and call centers in faraway lands create barriers between businesses and customers. An online search revealed over 10 ways to automate customer experiences with AI. Companies also outsource services to faraway places. Understanding the person on the other end of the line can be difficult. A business owner told the surprising story of calling the Department of Transportation. After the third ring a real human answered the phone. After learning of the problem, the human expressed empathy with the caller and transferred the call to another person who answered right away. After listening to the business owner, the human rephrased his concern, assured him the problem would be resolved and gave a date for a resolution. The owner smiled while telling the story because it is so unusual these days. We nodded in total agreement.

5. Showing Respect

"Do unto others as you would have them do unto you."

It is difficult to show respect when dealing with a snarky client or someone who raises their voice to get their way. However, treating customers the way we want to be treated goes a long way toward greater customer satisfaction and loyalty.

Facebook failed to respect consumer expectations. Data breaches affected millions of users, and fake news drove businesses and individuals away in a huge backlash. People remain angry about the company mishandling their private data. Wells Fargo is paying over $1 billion in fines after creating fake customer accounts, modifying mortgages without customer authorization, and charging customers for unnecessary insurance. The bank's growth was restricted by the Federal Reserve (Fed). Twitter (X) created a mass exodus of employees and consumers because of the disrespect shown to them by their new owner.

I served a client who complained about my fees and failed to follow through on homework assignments. Each meeting he complained, I smiled, nodded, and never defended myself. Finally, he said, "I know I need to do my assignments and want to continue using you." This client created a customer appreciation program to reward loyal customers. The strategy included client luncheons and personalized contact on birthdays and anniversaries. He began meeting weekly with his agents to improve communication, listened to their ideas, and ultimately increased sales. He listened more and more as his agency rose to third place in his market. Do not underestimate the power of respect shown to customers. A smile and nod of the head combined with being open to their ideas will move mountains.

6. Maintaining Consistency

Develop processes and procedures that exceed expectations. McDonald's became the juggernaut in the quick-service industry by standardizing meal production and service. Customers can count on the same experience in most McDonald's restaurants.

My wife reported that her favorite shop had closed. "It was no surprise," she said. "The pastries changed in consistency and taste over several months." I asked if the owner requested feedback on her recipe changes. This company went out of business because the owner changed her recipes and did not ask customers for feedback. Another pastry shop went out of business because it opened at random times of the morning. Customers could not count on getting a cup of coffee and a pastry on their way to work.

Customers abandon inconsistent services but remain loyal when they experience consistency in products and services and see smiling faces serving them. Lead your teams to create standardized processes for consistency and exceed expectations.

7. Getting Organized

Customers need to talk to people, not machines, when they need help. Competitive and resilient companies provide those serving customers with the ability to know their customers. My EV truck has a vehicle support team in Michigan. Any time I request services and follow-up, a different person answers. I repeat the same facts I shared before. The company's services would become more efficient and errors avoided if support services were located in service centers around the country, and staffed with service people assigned to designated territories and customer bases. The company would push services closer to customers and customers would receive higher levels of service.

8. Making Interactions Personal

Relying on technology to connect and communicate with customers builds barriers between companies, customers and consumers. "People are having difficulty having what I would describe as an authentic interaction," said Scott Broetzmann with Customer Care Measurement and Consulting. "Technology, for all of its benefits that it affords us, when it comes to having a problem and trying to get it resolved, in many cases it serves as an impediment," Broetzmann said. The reasonable solution is to keep human beings between the technology and customers. Use a person to answer phones and use people whose first language is the same as the language of the majority of the customer base. The temptation to use

CUSTOMERS AND TECHNOLOGY CHANGE 125

more technology for communicating with customers is how companies create barriers and discourage rather than delight customers.

9. Providing Accurate Information

Use technology to keep technology accurate. TechTonic Justice founder Kevin De Liban posts on his website that his firm has pioneered successful multidimensional advocacy strategies that win against unjust AI by blending litigation, community activation, public education, and media. They advertise that this battle-tested model will harness the strength of people on the ground to oppose unjust AI and those who insist on using it even where the harms are clear.

10. Setting Guardrails

Concerns are solvable with proper oversight. Until enough public pressure is applied to government officials to monitor and regulate artificial intelligence and social media, we will lag behind other countries that are acting responsibly with government regulation that protects public safety and privacy. As long as our officials create toothless regulation that is enforced by Big Tech, we will continue to be responsible for our own safety much like coal miners were before mine safety regulation (Box 12.2).

Box 12.2 How to delight customers

1. Ensuring quality
2. Gaining product knowledge
3. Providing rapid response
4. Communicating effectively
5. Showing respect
6. Maintaining consistency
7. Getting organized
8. Making interactions personal
9. Providing accurate information
10. Setting guardrails

The total solution for using social media and AI in business is facilitated best when companies build strong relationships with their representatives in state houses and U.S. congress with goals of establishing meaningful regulation. Regulation may sound like a dirty word, but as stated in the open letter from the Future Life Institute, businesses and Big Tech need to be on an even playing field. Sports at all levels have rules for how to play the game with referees to call violations. The same principle applies in business (including technology companies) as a governing body may serve technology as referees serve sporting events. Good news recently from San Francisco:

> SAN FRANCISCO—California Gov. Gavin Newsom signed a first-in-the-nation law on Monday that will force major AI companies to reveal their safety protocols—marking the end of a lobbying battle with big tech companies like ChatGPT maker OpenAI and Meta and setting the groundwork for a potential national standard.
>
> The measure, SB 53, requires some AI developers to publicly disclose their safety and security protocols. It also creates a way for companies and the public to report major safety incidents to the state. The law includes whistleblower protections for AI workers and lays the groundwork for a state-run cloud computing cluster dubbed CalCompute.
>
> (By Chase DiFeliciantonio, September 29, 2025,
> 04:20 p.m. EDT Updated: September 29, 2025,
> 06:38 p.m. EDT)

In summary, the uncertainty our companies and communities face, combined with the urgency to respond to adversity, makes it incumbent on business owners, leaders, and managers to consciously create an inclusive and collaborative culture to achieve resilience—just as the McDonald's team in Washington, DC, began competing, growing, and thriving. Just imagine what would happen if states competing for the same water source in drought conditions used the concepts outlined in this chapter. Imagine representatives meeting with a common vision and code of conduct. Their meeting agenda would focus on problem-solving issues and updating action plans in meetings. Communities and companies would fare better in today's demanding ecosystems. To assemble the puzzle pieces in this book, I offer the story of a client who adapted to the challenges of 2020 and turned around his business. While a smaller business, this leader experienced the same challenges as companies employing thousands of employees. His name is Tyler Richardson, agency manager of COUNTRY Financial, Tennessee. The story describes how Tyler adapted during the COVID-19 pandemic and became a respected leader in his company.

Five Questions

1. Building a business includes:
   A. Defining customer needs
   B. Building relationships
   C. Setting goals
   D. All of the above
2. Closing business deals does not include:
   A. Ask for agreement when detailing features
   B. Establish your qualifications at the beginning of the meeting
   C. Use names of satisfied clients
   D. Offer buying options
3. We do not delight customers with:
   A. Greater efficiency
   B. Specialty call centers
   C. Cycle time improvement
   D. Phone and Internet queries using humans
4. Which is true about customer call centers?
   A. Improve cycle time performance
   B. Save money
   C. Satisfy customers
   D. Effective use of AI

5. Which of the following is a company that delights customers?
   A. Facebook
   B. Wells Fargo
   C. Shark
   D. Twitter

Answers, Practices

Chapter 9   1 = B; 2 = B+D; 3 = C+D; 4 = B; 5 = C
Chapter 10   1 = C; 2 = C; 3 = A+C; 4 = C+D; 5 = C
Chapter 11   1 = A+C; 2 = D; 3 = D; 4 = B+C; 5 = A+B
Chapter 12   1 = D; 2 = B; 3 = B; 4 = B; 5 = C

PART 4

Transformation

How we consider the four disruptive forces when charting a new way forward leads to a resilient company with a brighter tomorrow. The degree that leaders are open to innovative ideas for renewing the mind, body, spirit, and soul of their organizations becomes the difference between barely surviving companies and resilient companies and communities. This story describes how any of us with an open mind can pull the parts of our companies together and swim against the currents in today's turbulence and uncertainty.

CHAPTER 13

Achieving Resilience

This story concerns a millennial whose business faced numerous challenges during the height of the COVID-19 pandemic, George Floyd social disruption, record number of climate disasters, and unbridled social media misinformation. I was introduced to this fine person by one of his agents who I had helped improve his business situation. As we began our journey, I asked Tyler Richardson, Agency Manager, COUNTRY Financial, Tennessee, a struggling insurance agency, to define his goals. Without hesitation, he described creating leaders in the agency, developing a leadership council and accountability, and creating top performers who could achieve challenging targets. Each of his goals was on target for responding to COVID-19 disruptions. His agency was underperforming, meeting only 29 percent of the company goals (home, auto, and life insurance sales) based on the sales production of 15 representatives (reps). Tyler's agency had fewer than 10 reps, but his assigned goals were based on the production of 15 reps. Over the next 20 weeks, Tyler adapted to making major changes to accomplish his goals during the turbulence of 2020 and 2021.

Getting Organized

Becoming a Coach

We reviewed and practiced the REACH coaching model: R is for developing rapport; E is establishing goals for a meeting; A represents the actions identified during ask, advise, and assist; C represents commitments made during a meeting; and H is having a record of the meeting.

Several options were discussed for designing the leadership council and decided on a structure that would include administrative help and a person from each agency office in the state. That was later revised to include a representative from each of three geographic regions of the state. Tyler's meetings were to include a flip chart and action list. As a leader, his new role was to first ask for ideas and only then offer his own. Tyler took the DISC survey to learn his work style. D is goal focused, I is people focused, S is process focused, and C is detail focused. Most of us have one or two main areas of focus but Tyler's focus was evenly distributed among all four attributes. He was uniquely suited to lead a diverse group of people. Tyler agreed to respond to a question with a question. For example, if asked for a solution, his first response would be, "What do you think?" If a rep asked to take a long weekend off, Tyler might ask, "Have you made your contacts for the week?" or "How have you prepared to get a good start next week?"

Board of Directors

The first decision for this newly formed board was to change its name from leadership council to board of directors (BOD). The directors then developed a structure consisting of three geographic regions (east, middle, and west). Each director would develop regional goals that supported state goals. "What would you think about conducting a culture survey to see how our reps see things?" Tyler asked. They agreed and chose to visit each region together as board members. Over the next few days, the directors presented the new structure in each region and reps were given time to react and ask questions. Afterward, Tyler contacted me to express pleasant surprise that everyone seemed excited to be part of a smaller and more connected group and accepted their regional leaders unconditionally. Tyler was reminded of the importance of recognizing any improvements made in the regions. We discussed having tokens such as gift cards and golf balls available in recognition of improvements when visiting offices and agreed on a Tennessee rebound retreat in July.

Productive Meetings

In our next coaching session, Tyler and I reviewed the key to successful collaboration is to have a regular time, location, and day of the week for meetings. A rule of thumb about how long to meet is based on meeting frequency: for example, one hour for a weekly meeting, two hours for two meetings per month, and four hours for a monthly meeting. The less frequent the meetings, the more items and problems to be resolved.

Agendas were created and sent to participants two days before meetings for their input. The agendas had times attached to each topic including recognition, action plan review, problem solving, and information sharing, followed by a meeting evaluation. The BOD decided to meet every other week for two hours. I also suggested that the BOD agree on goals for the state and that regional leaders establish goals for their regions with input from their reps. It was also important to keep in mind that there were both outcome measures and process measures. Outcome measures were sales numbers, while process measures were the number of calls made. State and region numbers should be considered outcome measures.

Balanced Scorecard

We planned the next BOD meeting. The idea was to create a statewide balanced scorecard. I advised the board to hang four flip chart pages on the wall and ask each director to identify statewide goals for each KPI. For example:

- Finance: Sales production as a percentage of the overall goal
- Operations: Implementing a new data system
- Customer satisfaction: Customer survey summary for the state
- Employee satisfaction: Culture survey results

I reminded Tyler of his accountability goal. He started instituting accountability when he counseled the two underperforming reps and with his intervention in the Franklin region dysfunction. Now was the time to build accountability across the state with balanced scorecards and action plans that tracked progress toward monthly and annual goals. His next meeting would focus on developing a balanced scorecard.

We discussed the value of tracking outcome measures for the scorecard. For example, not to count the number of sales calls; instead, count sales and the dollar value of sales for the week. A rep may want to count sales calls for their scorecard, but the state scorecard only measured outcomes. You may wonder why this is so important. Tyler's company emphasized process measures, and production was not moving at all. A rep can call on everyone in the world but still have lousy sales numbers. Measuring the outcome—in this case sales—gives an accurate picture of actual performance. I found that reminding the BOD several times was necessary for them to understand how this change in culture could make a difference in business outcomes.

Accountability

Low Sales Performance

Our next meeting goal was to resolve the low sales performance of two reps and to plan for his first leadership meeting. We reviewed the "When You" corrective feedback model for improving performance and the importance of following up with positive reinforcement when improvements occurred. This model is a tool for being assertive rather than aggressive when correcting behavior. These reps' low sales figures were significant contributors to the 29 percent productivity in Tennessee.

During the week, Tyler conducted performance reviews with both reps: for example, "John, when you project high sales numbers that don't occur, our agency numbers remain low, frustrating me and my boss. What are you going to do to match your rosy projections with actual sales?" He noted each rep's responses and recorded their actions for weekly review. The process revealed that one person had a reading disorder. Tyler reassigned him to a job he could perform. The other rep resigned.

Group Dysfunction

Tyler was concerned about the Franklin, Tennessee region. It was beset with complaints, excuses, and low performance. Reps were jealous of one another and did not accept responsibility for not accomplishing their own goals, much less regional or state ones. We discussed an intervention plan:

- Call a meeting with all reps, together with Joe, the regional director.
- Take a flip chart to Franklin to facilitate the meeting.

- Decide on questions for the meeting in advance.
- Keep in mind that the role of Joe and Tyler was to ask questions; no solutions or discussion from them unless asked.
- List on the chart all issues described by the group; using round-robin facilitation to reduce tension and ensure that everyone had an opportunity to speak.
- List issues raised in the exact words used by participants. Reviewing all items when the group had run out of ideas.
- Use the 80/20 rule to vote for 20 percent of the most pressing issues and entering them on an action plan worksheet with the names of reps who volunteered to address each one.
- Let the group know they would return in two weeks to review the action plan and sales performance.

Two weeks later Tyler was back in Franklin. This time, reps were laughing and let him know that their issues had been resolved and that oh, by the way, sales were up!

Concerning Tyler's leadership council, we planned topics for the meeting and organized the council with representatives from each regional market. Each leader had been chosen based on sales production and their ability to relate with other reps. One of the first duties of the council would be to conduct a culture for success survey across the state's offices. The council's clear focus was to move the state's productivity from 29 to 100 percent by year-end.

Growing People and Business

Developing Leaders

I reviewed with Tyler four decision-making options, including *Direct, Involve, Engage,* and *Empower.* Direct decisions applies when the leader is the only person with knowledge or when decisions must be made rapidly in an emergency such as a climate disaster.

Involve decisions are used to solicit ideas from the team before making the final decision. Better-informed decisions happen, and leaders gain more support from workers. Engage decisions are used when everyone in the group is impacted by the decision. For example, a hurricane is anticipated. The leader gathers their staff to decide what supplies and equipment will be needed to secure their building from the storm. Everyone will be impacted by this decision so the leader acts as a team member when discussing and deciding on what to get and how to use it. The whole team is prepared to obtain supplies and use the equipment. Empower decisions occur when the leader delegates the decision to the group.

Three ways to brainstorm ideas with a group were reviewed. Round-robin is used to ensure everyone is heard by going around the table calling on members to share ideas. Freewheeling involves posing a question and encouraging ideas to come randomly from group members. The slip method uses posted notes for participants to write their thoughts and then attached to a flip chart or whiteboard. I reminded Tyler that his role was to be a facilitator of decisions rather than the sole decision maker. He was getting more comfortable with the idea. We touched on the importance of asking open questions, repeating the message being heard, and offering an empathy statement.

We practiced using problem solving to overcome obstacles and reach higher sales volumes. We reviewed five steps:

1. Identify the problem in measurable terms.
2. Define all causes of the problem.
3. Identify solutions to critical causes.
4. Create an action plan using the solutions.
5. Implement and evaluate success.

We chose a real problem, low financial sales: life insurance is 20 percent of goal of 100. We then developed solutions within an hour. Tyler's assignment was to use what he had just practiced with his BOD at the next meeting.

Increasing Production

What makes us do the things we do? Tyler and I reviewed the fact that all behavior happens because of punishment or positive reinforcement. When we rely on punishment and threats, company performance is mediocre. Conversely, positive reinforcement encourages higher levels of individual and group performance. We discussed how human resources systems are ineffective motivators since feedback on performance occurs once or twice a year. When developing a plan to correct behavior, we learned the difference between can't-do and won't-do behavior. John's learning disability is an example of can't do. Harry can sell policies but does not. That is a won't-do behavior and requires a different solution.

Four times more positive feedback than corrective was reviewed as a proven tool for increasing productivity. However, do not mix corrective feedback with positive feedback unless training someone or giving a performance review. To reverse low performance in won't-do situations like Harry, the tool for increasing sales is with approving comments as their sales improve. We discussed how Tyler could reinforce board members and reps and the importance of ensuring his people knew that outings and other recognition were earned by improving or achieving their goals.

Tyler and the BOD began applying this idea to life insurance sales. They developed a graph measuring daily and weekly life insurance sales and called it the "Road to 100." The graph was published every time a sale occurred and the person making the sale was recognized statewide. Their goal was 100 life insurance policy sales by the end of the year. They sold 110 policies in three months. The BOD was learning the power of positive reinforcement.

Business Strategy

The work on a balanced scorecard for the agency was a prequel to the plan for a rebound retreat that would include everyone in Tyler's Tennessee-based agency. This was the final step as Tyler adapted how he led to create his agency of leaders during the difficulties created by the COVID-19 pandemic. Tyler swam upstream during this time by pulling everyone together against all odds.

We met in Gatlinburg. The evening before the retreat everyone assembled after supper to share DISC profiles, culture survey results, discuss the events of the coming day, and receive encouraging words from Tyler. The following day the group convened in a conference room nearby. Tyler's reps met in their new regional teams with their leaders. Tyler shared the challenges the agency was experiencing and anticipating over the course of the year.

A miracle happened. Tyler asked each table to determine production goals for the remainder of the year. Understand, this is an insurance company; people are told what their goals are by leaders they may have never met. Tyler totally shifted the goal-setting paradigm by asking his reps to set their own goals. After their reports and a break, they moved around the room in pairs sharing their ideas for improving their numbers on the region's financials, operations, employee turnover, and clients to achieve their production goals. After lunch the teams completed their lists and action plans. Each team leader reported their plans and Tyler shared how their contributions would impact statewide production goals. He later confided to me that their goals were more aggressive than he would have expected them to achieve. He was ecstatic! So was I!

Tyler adapted and transformed his low-producing insurance agents into a high-performing and competitive agency of leaders. Using the tools and talents of engagement and involvement, he created leaders across his business, as seven out of 10 of his reps attained all-star status. His agency became a top producer in COUNTRY Financial's wider U.S. marketplace. He created greater capacity as his team of 10 achieved goals set for 15 representatives. When I sent him his diploma, Tyler responded, "Thanks, Ron! This is something I am incredibly proud of and I'm thankful that I committed to going through your program. We are reaching milestones that have never been achieved in the history of this agency, and it all started when we started working together."

I hope the contents in this book stimulate ideas for instituting resilient practices when dealing with the next challenge coming your way. We know we will be affected sooner rather than later by destructive forces and are well served by remaining alert as we anticipate uncertainty. A living strategy updated monthly and revised annually can lead to brighter futures when confronted by four increasingly disruptive forces. Take a few minutes to complete resilient practices on the next page to begin building your great and resilient company.

As I reflect on those leaders who struggle while others move confidently through choppy waters, I remain hopeful that we learn from one another by listening and planning together in order to navigate our businesses and communities to bright and sustainable futures. The manner in which we use compassion, collaboration, and knowledge can build great organizations in today's turbulent world.

Resilient Practices

Place a check mark against each item to indicate whether your organization performs the practice consistently (Table 13.1).

More than 28 yes answers indicate you are building a great organization. Less than 28 yes answers imply you have opportunities to use compassion, collaboration, and knowledge to build resilience into your organization and gain market share.

Table 13.1 Resilient practices

Leadership	Yes	No
Leaders and management practice communication, collaboration, motivation, and innovation with peers and employees.		
Problem solving rather than blaming is practiced at work.		
Work is balanced with personal lives.		
Practices are in place for reducing and stabilizing employee turnover.		
Managers have been trained to meet regularly with their teams and facilitate decision making and problem solving.		
Disruption		
We have plans in place and anticipate climate disasters in our community.		
We communicate with our representatives about their voting patterns and impact on our communities and companies.		
We are aware of labor availability and talent in our community.		
We have regular reviews of technology innovations and impact to our companies.		
We have teams to monitor and offer an analysis of the four disruptive forces.		
Business Model		
We conduct an annual analysis of our markets and consider innovative actions to gain market share.		
Strategy is developed with input from management, staff, customers, and suppliers.		
Our strategy is reviewed monthly and updated annually.		
Scorecards measuring financials, operations, employee satisfaction, and customer satisfaction are visible throughout the company.		
Our strategy includes actions and reactions to climate disasters, political actions, social complexity, and technology change.		

(continued)

Table 13.1 Resilient practices (continued)

Leadership	Yes	No
Operations		
We have mastermind teams throughout our company.		
Our teams meet weekly to review progress on projects.		
Our teams focus on improving efficiency, reducing waste and costs.		
Our processes are regularly reviewed seeking ways to increase efficiency.		
Our teams focus on improving company scorecards and goals.		
Finance		
Company values/ethics are posted in highly visible work areas.		
Company financials are regularly shared with all employees.		
Employees provide input in company budgets and financial decisions.		
Employees are empowered to find innovative solutions to increasing profit margins.		
Employees share in company financial improvements.		
Employees		
There is four times more positive feedback than corrective feedback at work.		
Pay equity is monitored to ensure genders and cultures are paid equitably for their work.		
Performance reviews are based on company and team scorecard outcomes and goal attainment.		
Workers are trained to work together and use new technologies and products.		
Upskilling and reskilling programs are in place using adult learning principles		
Customers		
Customer feedback is solicited after every transaction.		
Customer calls are answered by a human.		
Customer complaints are remedied rapidly and accurately by humans.		
Company focus is doing it right the first time.		
Employees are trained to communicate effectively with customers.		
Total number of yes/no responses		

About the Author

Ron Robinson has consulted with companies as far north and south as Winnipeg, Canada, to San Juan, Puerto Rico; as far east and west as Taiwan to Orange County, California. He has spoken to audiences as large as 3,000 and facilitated groups as large as 300 participants. He has assessed and turned around Fortune 500 enterprises, midsize companies and entrepreneurs starting their own businesses. Ron wrote *On All Cylinders: Succeeding as an Entrepreneur and a Leader*, which has been instrumental in helping a number of small and midsize businesses become highly resilient and successful during the COVID-19 pandemic. The disruptions in 2020 became the catalyst for the constant drumbeat of change and uncertainty companies and communities must contend with to survive and thrive. *Practices of Resilient Companies: Overcome Disruption with Compassion, Collaboration, and Knowledge* has been written to provide a business model for companies and nonprofits to become resilient and succeed in the choppy economy we experience today.

A graduate of the University of North Carolina, with a BS in industrial relations, Ron is certified and experienced using lean manufacturing, total quality management, strategic planning, and leadership development to aid companies rise in their market and overcome the troubles they face. Industries served include financial services, publication, transportation, health care, nonprofits, software development, and manufacturing.

Growing up in the South, Ron became a storyteller early in his career. He remains active as a speaker offering engaging presentations to leaders of organizations and associations. He enjoys hiking with his wife, Judy, and Harvey their Labrador Retriever, when exploring the Appalachian Mountains. He can be contacted for interactive presentations by e-mail at mountainronrobinson@gmail.com. For more details, please scan the QR code.

Index

www.ingramcontent.com/pod-product-compliance
Lightning Source LLC
Chambersburg PA
CBHW061508180526
45171CB00001B/91